D0707986

Half the World's People

Half the World's People

G. Alison Raymond

Appleton-Century-Crofts
Division of Meredith Publishing Company, New York

Library of Congress Card Number: 65-20559

Printed in the United States of America

695-2

To my sister,
whose unfailing interest in my work
means more to me than she
will ever understand

Why This Book Was Written

"Man is tied to all men, as all men are tied to him, in a web whose threads no eye can follow, and no fingers can unravel."

JUDGE LEARNED HAND, 1930

To write about "Half The World's People" may seem presumptuous. How can anyone be so bold as to attempt such a task? Yet:

> Despite the striking but superficial differences of clothing, food, houses, or speech
> Despite the deeper differences of religious faith, cultural experience, family relationships, attitudes towards work, or political beliefs

I believe that that half of the world's people who happen to be women have basically the same concerns, the same hopes for their children, the same kinds of contribution to make to their nations. This I believe is true whether they live in New York, Helsinki, Teheran, Dar es Salaam, Rio de Janeiro, Madras, or Singapore.

Their concerns include such universal matters as:

Spiritual strength.
Peace and disarmament.
Racial, religious, tribal, caste, and class barriers.
Morality and integrity in government, business, and personal life.
The place of tradition in a changing world.
Fast-growing cities, with all their dislocations and problems.
Population growth.
Shortage of teachers and overcrowded schools.
Increasing juvenile delinquency.
Changing family patterns.
Spiraling costs of living.

In the belief that all women share these same deep concerns, this book is written. At least in some small measure, I hope that it will help to do three things:

1. Clarify the remarkable social changes that are rapidly affecting people throughout the world.
2. Show how women's lives are being changed by these world currents.
3. Show how women are *causing* change and how singly, together, and side by side with men, they can contribute further to a more stable world.

With Heartfelt Thanks

The process of writing even a small book makes one deeply conscious of how dependent each one of us is on a multitude of other people.

One's thoughts, one's point of view, one's examples, and one's sources are all influenced constantly by conversations, by books, or by experiences made possible through other people's kindness.

Therefore I cannot express my full appreciation and indebtedness. I can mention only a few people while deeply aware of how much necessarily remains unexpressed to many other groups and individuals. They, too, have helped—consciously or unconsciously—in the writing of this book. These include people in many parts of the world who kindly read and commented on earlier drafts, many who contributed examples and suggested points, many whose words I have quoted. I have tried to mention all the latter to the best of my ability. If I have missed giving credit to anyone for written or spoken words that I have absorbed, it is unintentional, and I hope will be forgiven.

I should like to express special appreciation, however, to:

My parents—who, from my earliest remembrance, created in me a sense of the wholeness of the world.

Miss Ruth Woodsmall—whose shining faith in the world's women has had profound influence on me.

The Committee of Correspondence—with whom I worked for many years. The Committee gave me opportunities, experiences, memories, and friendships throughout the world which I cherish. Without these, this book could never have been written.

Contents

Part One

What Can Be Done

❁

One

Grandmother, Mother, and Now?

When I was a child, it was a real journey to go beyond the next town. We went by horse and buggy, of course. Naturally you could not pick up the phone and call your friend either, because there was no phone. So you wrote a note. It took a day or two to get an answer to even the simplest question.

We never knew what was happening in other parts of the world. When we finally did, it was so late that we knew things must have changed in the meantime. That made other parts of the world seem detached and far away.

It has been during my lifetime that all those gadgets have been invented to reduce household tasks. But you know, in a way, I think it was easier for mothers in those earlier days despite the modern so-called "labor-saving devices." Maiden aunts and grandmothers always seemed to be available then to help with the children. It is hard for me to see how today's young mothers manage.

I was already grown-up before we moved out of the leisurely horse-drawn pace of my childhood. But look what has happened since! You can reach any spot in the world in a matter of hours! Imagine hearing live voices from Japan, Egypt, and the Congo, and will we ever get used to seeing those men's faces on screens in our own living rooms?

THIS WAS MY mother talking. The incredible change from kerosene lamp to astronaut took place during the life of her generation—the past fifty years. That same kind of extraordinary change in pace, mobility, and family life is taking place now in most parts of the world.

We in the West have had fifty years in which to adapt. It is hard for us to understand the enormity of the problems facing the great majority of today's people who are now radically changing their ways of life not in fifty years, but in five, or fifteen.

Take the question of language, for example. There are said to be about eight hundred languages in Africa alone. When people remained in tight tribal groups, this created no major difficulties. But now, as they move about, as schools draw children together, as planes open up hitherto remote regions, this diversity of tongues is a real problem. Imagine what difficulties of conversation there must be in road-building teams, in industrial plants, in training programs, in hospital wards!

Humans everywhere share a basic need to feel secure. This fundamental is shaken when social patterns suddenly rearrange themselves like the turn of a kaleidoscope without sufficient time for adjustment. What was secure suddenly crumbles; what was a pattern is suddenly a snarl; what was morally acceptable suddenly is not; what was sacred is suddenly empty. This leads to an unsettled, searching, restless and, at times, defensive feeling.

Among the major difficulties lies the fact that cultures, like the people they produce, have their superstitions which hold them back and make adjustment difficult.

Dr. Mohei-el-Din Saber, writing on obstacles to progress in the Arab World, points up this kind of conflict of spirit:

> It is . . . impossible to admit the presence of microbes and at the same time quote the old saying that "He who has suffered an illness is wiser than a doctor"; to accept the necessity

of a banking system, while believing that interest is wrong or sinful; to educate women, then to insist on their wearing the veil or keeping them at home.[1]

What happens as events move faster than traditions?

For one thing, reverence for age wavers. It is the young leaders who understand the new movements. They begin to draw the ear of young villagers. Literate youth, rather than illiterate age, is called upon to interpret events.

The very roots of social balance may be affected by new values as these spread throughout the world. New values demand new kinds of behavior that clash with traditions. Not everybody wants to change. The idea is new, for example, that services such as health care, housing, and education should be offered to individuals and that a community has an obligation to provide them. This is hard for people to comprehend in vast areas of the world where each family has, since time began, lived and died on its own, not in any sense the responsibility of some impersonal "community planner."

Look at the elements which make up society. These include not only the educated in the cities but also the Bedouin living in his tent of camel's hair, the almost naked man of the bush, the peasant believing more in his amulets than in antibiotics. Millions of people live far below what is nowadays considered an acceptable standard, but what changes must occur in sets of values before such people can readily accept improved housing, standardized clothes, balanced diets, and proper medical services.

Happiness is a subtle thing, deeply entwined with the aims and goals which govern a person's life and how successful he is in reaching them. The changes that planners have in mind to raise standards of living may cause tensions and disturb the very fabric of life for many categories of people. Change and what is considered "progress" do not necessarily come easily.

Urban growth causes profound social upheavals. All over the world men flock to cities seeking work. They once lived in communities where everybody knew them. Their behavior was everybody's business because the whole town knew the family and watched the child grow up. Suddenly, in a city, each person becomes anonymous. Nobody cares any longer about him. Every kind of new temptation surrounds him. The fixed rights and wrongs of his earlier, simpler life become confused and faint.

Single women, too, crowd into cities, seeking new lives. They are not merely looking for men but they, too, want interest and life, as well as a livelihood. Single working women are still looked on with suspicion by their elders in many lands. Public approval and acceptance of new kinds of life come slowly. On the whole, today's changes are harder for women than for men because women must adjust from a far more restricted past.

Where are single girls going to live in the cities? Where are they going to learn marketable skills such as typing, bookkeeping, or handling a bobbin?

How are they to maintain moral standards if they have neither job nor family, nor a decent place to live?

What happens to people when they leave the land of their forebears, but can find no job?

The whole focus of life is changing for women in country after country. A woman from Korea writes:

> When we became independent, women began to realize their responsibility to the country, as well as to raise their own position. They realize how important it is that they take part in their country's growth. They no longer like to depend on husbands only.

In my grandmother's day life took place within four walls. My grandmother had to obey three men during her lifetime: her father, her husband, and her eldest son. She had no rights —to anything. . . . But since the liberation in 1945, the shift in the world has brought a great change to Korean women. Now most girls intend to get jobs after school, though the door to jobs is still narrow.[2]

Pannini Rudaravanija, of Thailand, said:

The biggest change happened for us in 1921 when a law was passed that said ALL children between the ages of seven and twelve must go to school. This conflicted with the old belief that women should be kept at home, so it took a while to come about. But once girls began to go to school, women realized their own abilities and began to do many things.

Now what do you suppose? Of all the college graduates in our country, over 38 per cent are women, the highest percentage in Asia. And do you know what it is in USA? Only 35 per cent. Finland has the highest record in the world, with 44 per cent. Then comes Thailand; we are second in the world. See what happens when girls can go to school![3]

Not only in Korea are women moving out of a four-walled existence; not only in Thailand are girls accompanying their brothers to school. The same could now be said of women in most countries of the world.

Technical changes in a land are the easiest to see—the magic of telephones, radios, hydroelectric power, air conditioning, and jets. The fruits of such tangible developments are as yet reaching relatively few. The great majority of the world's people still walk behind their ancient plows, feeling the dust on their bare feet, or carry heavy loads on weary heads and backs. But electricity is stalking on great pylons across more and more of the earth's surface; roads are going up mountains and winding down through valleys; radios are bringing new ideas to millions. Even on the loneliest farms, families gather to hear broadcasts bounced back to them miraculously from outer space.

One revolutionary idea that is rocking today's world is the sudden realization everywhere, after generations of patient acceptance, that *things need not always be so hard.* The poor need not always be so poor. The hungry hear the word and know their children need not die from hunger. This new awareness strikes at the very soul of man. It is not radio, nor electricity, nor speed, but today's determination for rapid change that is the most extraordinary differcnce between our time and that of our grandmothers.

Throughout Asia, where more than half the world's people live, the average farmer has a few acres of land. He is usually his own beast of burden—or more often his wife is. They carry on their backs the produce they have raised to sell and the meager supplies they take back, after market, to their small farm. Living is an endless, exhausting round. The farm home is just a place to eat a thin meal, then fall asleep on a hard floor bed before the next day's work. But, despite the monotony, awareness grows. Many now have access to radios in their villages. Current news is seeping in; so are music and new ideas.

People are starting to think beyond their tiny village circle. If you ask a woman in a remote village in the mountains of northern Greece, or a long-haired peasant in the Andes, or a *fellahin* along the Nile, "What do you want for your children?" he will reply:

"School."

"Why?"

"So their lives will be better than this."

For many centuries the world's millions did not conceive that their children's lives *could* be different from their own

Now they do. Despite natural human conservatism and the preaching of some leaders who deplore change, most of the world's people see hope ahead for themselves and their children.

There are profound difficulties which often make progress a complicated matter.

An American social scientist traveling the village areas of Iraq sought an answer to the question: "Even where villagers *are* eager for change, why is it so difficult to establish new ideas?"

On his return he reported:

> One clue lies in the fact . . . that the villagers are waiting for government, or some other outside agency, to bring about this imperfectly understood "progress." They thus do nothing to advance progress themselves, rather, they passively accept the innovation and once the agency of change is removed they lapse as often as not into the old way of doing things.[4]

Sometimes change is wanted, but the by-products that come with it are not. This, too, can create disturbances. The father may be pleased when his educated daughter gets a job, but less pleased when, in her new freedom, she wants to choose her own husband. Or the worker who talks loudly in the village about his own "powerful nation" may not, when it comes to the point, want personally to undergo the discipline of regular and long factory hours to help build his nation's strength.

For some communities there is a groping desire for change, but no leader. No one has any initiative. They may be dragged down by disease, or exhausted by the daily round of life, or destroyed by village jealousies and rivalries. Others want the "something better" which they know is within their reach, but experience, with its harsh lessons, has made them shrewd. Life has taught them to be wary of letting go what little they have. They reach only slowly and tentatively for the new while holding fast, at the same time, to the familiar.

There is no wonder that today's world is undergoing great upheavals. Some of the concerns with which mankind is struggling are of a magnitude never faced before. Life is more precarious than it has ever been. This is true because, for the first time, man now has the power to war against that which is God's. Not only can he kill man, but now he can change his very body and nature by the weapons he has created. His painful attempts at peace become crucial and urgent as man tries:

> To develop new harmonies among nations which scarcely know or understand each other.
> To remove chilling threats of destruction.
> To replace colonial dependencies or feudal rulers by responsible citizenship.
> To remove the hunger, poverty, and disease which has plagued humanity since the beginning of recorded history.

One of the marvels of our time is the way in which men of many nations are working together more and more to help each other.

Icelanders, Swedes, Norwegians, Canadians, Japanese—all skilled fishing folk—have, for example, gone to India. There, in a school near Bombay, they are teaching young fishermen to harvest the sea in new ways, thus helping to feed a hungry land. Similarly, the Nationalist Chinese, who grow the highest yield of rice per hectare of any in the world, are passing this vital skill on to Liberia and Libya, to Paraguay, Brazil, and the Dominican Republic. Last year, forty-nine Africans from nineteen countries traveled all the way to Taiwan for several months of class and field training in rice-growing.

In thousands of such training programs taking place all over the globe, the world's unskilled are steadily working in ever-greater numbers to become skilled and therefore raise the standard of life and income wherever they may be.

A group in Malaysia amused themselves by itemizing the international elements in their daily lives.

> Our tea is from Ceylon; the rice is from Thailand or Burma; the films we see are from USA, China, India, or Japan; our cloth is woven in Lancashire, Benares, or Kelantan; the chocolates our children eat may have been the product of both Kenya and Britain; our babies' milk comes from Switzerland.
>
> Even more important is how connected we all are. What takes place in Cuba has effects in Asia; the conflict between India and China matters in the United States; the Berlin Wall affects all Europe; even in South America it makes a difference.[5]

Every country owes a debt to others in one field or another. None need feel either superior or inferior, for no nation, new or old, grows and prospers without aid from others during its development. As Will Rogers, the American humorist and philosopher, said, "All of us are ignorant, only fortunately we are ignorant about different things."

Today, while many lands are striving to modernize, western countries, too, are searching for new directions that will affect us all. In universities and laboratories, in council meetings and board rooms, exploring minds are hard at work. Change is measured not only in terms of plows and irrigation ditches and refrigerators. It is measured even more in attitudes and ideas.

Look at Western Europe. For centuries man has tried to unite Europe by force and bloodshed. During the past twenty years more unity has come quietly to Western Europe than has existed since the days of the Roman Empire. This has come about through the power of an idea, a change in man's attitude, a new willingness to co-operate with his fellow man.

The *revolution of rising expectations* in Western Europe is leading it toward economic unity and perhaps, eventually, to political unity. Although businessmen by the score once said that it could not possibly succeed, Europe's Common Market is actually moving ahead. The smoking chimneys of productive factories, the press of traffic, the steady stream of loaded freight trains steaming across Europe make a prosperous vitality plain for all to see.

The job is by no means done. It is an extremely difficult task which has suffered a number of staggering disappointments and setbacks. Nevertheless, the idea of unity, toward which Europe is steadily working, is one of enormous consequence to all the world.

Victor Hugo once said, "There is nothing so powerful as an idea whose hour has come." National independence has been this kind of powerful idea in our time. The practice of free nations grouping together voluntarily for strength is another powerful idea which appears to be gathering momentum. Western Europe is painfully hammering out its new and broader grouping to benefit its members. African leaders meet together frequently to work out African alliances. Long negotiations created a new grouping of Malaysian territories. With less internal competition, larger markets, and greater unity, nations can achieve greater prosperity, which will hopefully be reflected in the lives of their people.

The steps that various countries are taking to improve their peoples' lot will, no doubt, be adapted by other nations in ways to fit their own specific needs. Countries will learn from one another's mistakes and one another's triumphs. The idea of passionate nationalism may yield to broader inter-regional and international concepts as communications bring the world closer together.

During its relatively brief history, the United States has contributed a number of powerful ideas which are still having their quiet effects throughout much of the world. Constitutions of many lands are based on the concept, first conceived by the early settlers of the United States, that it is possible to have a republic—a government "of the people, by the people, for the people"—over a vast geographic area. This had not been tried before except in small communities.

Another revolutionary American concept has made possible one of the greatest democratic processes in all history. This is the idea that every child, regardless of his economic status, is worth educating by free, tax-supported schools. Since the early days of covered wagons, the people of the United States have been able to change their status—to move ahead on their own merits and abilities, without regard to class, or rank, or family wealth. This social mobility has helped to build the United States in under two hundred years from a land of primeval forest and open plain grazed by roaming buffalo, to what it is today. The job of providing full equality and human dignity for all people is as yet far from accomplished in the United States. However, the ideals are there, toward which the majority of people in the nation are striving. Many of these same ideals have been borrowed, adapted, and made part of the thinking of other lands.

Today the United States is still experimenting, still changing, still restlessly seeking new patterns of life. No doubt these new ideas will have varied effects in other parts of the world. Some of today's experiments concern automation, which may, to some extent, take drudgery out of man's life. If, as predicted, machines take over nine-tenths of his work, what will happen to today's accepted values? As the work of unskilled or semiskilled workers is taken over, what will be used as the measure of man's worth, in place of the old familiar concept of a "good day's work"?

Other new directions of thought in western countries include: the reduction of illness, pain, hunger, and poverty; the elimination of the evils of slums and city sprawl for urban millions; the provision of cultural outlets for more people through orchestras, recordings, paperback books, folk festivals, and the like.

In addition, probing, searching minds are stretching out to explore space, to plumb the oceans' depths, to plunge under Arctic ice. Constant and profound efforts are being made to lessen tensions and to find a peaceful road where wars will be no more.

There are still places where there appears to be little desire for change, as in parts of Indonesia or the Caribbean Islands where people are blessed by a warm climate and ample food. Life is pleasant. Why change? But in most areas where nature is not kind, where villages lack food and water, where people struggle to secure even the barest essentials, hope that things *can* be different stirs men's souls. So does it in Birmingham, Alabama, or Harlem, New York.

Change comes at a varying pace; some of it good, some bad. It has always been a basic element in life. Today it appears to be particularly explosive, affecting every one of us, wherever we may live.

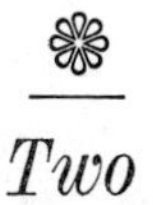

Two

Families and Men

A GROUP OF WOMEN in East Pakistan were discussing why the joint family pattern is changing so quickly in their part of the world.

"Widespread movement is breaking up families," this group agreed, "but this is not the primary reason for the break-up of the system. More fundamental is the rising cost of living. Heads of houses can no longer afford to feed and clothe, let alone educate, the families of brothers and cousins. It is all they can do to look after their own immediate families in terms fitting their own new ideas, because these ideals are changing. Nowadays, men want to give more opportunity and education to their own children than they once did."[1]

Writes a Malaysian:

> Twenty years ago my father—eldest brother and filial son—cared for his father, supported and educated his sister, his own twelve children, his third brother's ten others, and kept an eye on his youngest brother's two. Today his twelve children, mostly married, limit their families to two or three children and, although very closely knit, make it clear that they will not be responsible for *their* brothers' and sisters' families, let alone their cousins'.
>
> Generally speaking, the aged and the unemployed are still

looked after. But in another decade or two, will it be the same? Recognizing this, the older woman of Asia is beginning to change her outlook somewhat. She no longer feels quite so secure in the thought that her son's home will inevitably be hers, and she wonders whether she will reign there supreme as did *her* mother-in-law. Today she is beginning to make provision for herself; husbands, too, consider their wives' possible widowhood in a way that used not to be true when it was assumed that the son would necessarily take over the responsibility.[2]

External changes and basic readjustments are major factors in twentieth-century life. Despite this, one fundamental truth remains which has been set forth clearly by the United Nations Declaration of Human Rights: "The family is the natural and fundamental unit of society."

No matter what else she may also be called upon to do, woman's most essential function will always be as guardian of the family. Women should be giving fresh thought and careful study therefore to various basic questions that affect the family in today's world:

Should divorce be made easier or more difficult? Why? Does it give women more security when divorce is hard to get, or is she better off when divorce is easy?

Are trial marriages desirable or definitely not desirable? Would marriage be more secure or less secure if the partners had known each other better in advance? To what extent?

What about polygamy? Do the advantages of shelter, a home, a sense of solidarity and avoidance of the stigma of spinsterhood outweigh the disadvantages?

As women's economic position changes and she goes out to work, what happens to the traditional man-woman relationship? Are marriages based on the same values that they used to be? If not, what are the new values?

These, and questions like them, should be under thoughtful discussion all over the world—by men as well as women. They are fundamental to newly evolving family patterns.

At Addis Ababa in 1960, African women from thirty-one countries considered polygamy and agreed that it was "undesirable and outmoded." "It does not make for a stable family life," they reported, "but creates an environment where rivalry, deceit, and distrust flourish—a harmful atmosphere for children."[3]

They raised problems of support for the children of cast-off wives, and then stated, "A serious consequence of polygamy in rural areas of Africa is that a few wealthy older men number within their family groups most of the marriageable girls of the district so the younger men cannot find wives." They considered this to be one cause of the drift to towns by unmarried young men and one reason for the growth of prostitution in the towns.

Writing of the Arab world, Morroe Berger discusses the relationships within families and between man and woman.[4] He says that for Arab families, a pervading feature is the strong code governing relations between the sexes. Women's premarital chastity is of the highest value, as is their marital fidelity. Transgression in these areas is punished by severe disgrace, sometimes by banishment, in some traditional communities even by death. He points out that marriage in the Arab world is still primarily a joining of two families, rather than of two individuals; therefore infidelity on the part of a woman affronts not only her husband, but both families. It is normally the woman's father and brothers, rather than her husband, who administer the penalty for the disgrace she has caused.

Within the family circle the older generations tend to shape family life for the younger. Men's desires and values are still more important than those of women, and must be given major consideration. For centuries, Oriental women have been trained to be subordinate to men, to remain secluded in their own world, to please men and cultivate their own femininity. Men resist such matters as adoption of western dress, which "exposes" the woman. They do not like her to move freely about in public or to accept employment outside the home.

Yet, in their desire for national strength, Mr. Berger notes, men are welcoming the basic processes which lead to the emancipation of women—primarily, education and industrialization. Because of these pervasive new elements in life, Arab women are moving towards an equality their mothers never knew. In general, men find it easier to be convinced of the value of independence for their daughters than for their wives; they are more willing to let them be educated, move about, and have a greater sense of independence. The generation now growing up, therefore, will see enormous changes.

Mr. Berger concludes by saying:

> If forces already set in train are permitted to work out their potentialities, or, as is likely, even to become more pronounced, there is no doubt that women's aspirations, demands, and successes will transform Arab society profoundly and permanently.[5]

Writing of the United States, where family patterns are also changing, Melissa Redfield says:

> The American passion for collecting and publishing statistics has made [the American] divorce rate famous, but [many] would argue that we chose in this century to make divorce easier precisely because of the high value we place on a good marriage. . . . It is also true that most divorcees remarry and the percentage of married women has steadily increased.[6]

In his book *Her Infinite Variety* Morton Hunt points out:

> Europeans . . . especially those from the Mediterranean countries, find it remarkable and even laughable that American men so rarely have mistresses, and American women so rarely have lovers. The Frenchman or Italian may suppose this is so because Americans are inhibited, awkward, and puritanical about love, and in part he is right. . . . Incomprehensible as it may seem to the Gallic or Italian mind, the American's wife is something of a mistress to him, as he is something of a lover to her.[7]

People of various cultures look at marriage and at divorce in various ways, but the new mobility, new family structures, opportunities for new educational levels for girls as well as boys, all have a bearing on marriage relationships. In every family the wife is an influence one way or the other—for good or for evil; she can be a "carrier" or a "barrier"; she can help or hinder.

Miss Edith Dlamini of South Africa tells the story of a man who saw a ragged, thin, little refugee boy scrabbling for garbage to eat. When asked where his parents were, he pointed to a miserable tar-paper shack. "What a pity that you have no home," said the man. The boy looked up quickly. "Oh, we do have a home," he said. "We just don't have a house to put it in." What a mother he must have!

Traditionally women do not like change. They tend to be conservative. They would rather have things remain the way their parents and grandparents had them. But this is not to be. Modern changes may or may not be desirable, but nonetheless, they are coming. Women who are ready to adapt, understand, and enjoy—ready to do what their husbands want, rather than hold back—can ease the transitions of family life.

It is hard for people to adjust to new roles, totally different from those in which they were trained. In an orthodox Chinese family, for example, a man must first be a filial son, then a responsible brother. He must respect and revere his parents, care for his brother and often his brother's family. This is what he learns from childhood. Nowadays, however, he often goes to an English or American school and absorbs the western outlook. Here he is taught to cleave to his wife, to love and cherish her first. When her demands and those of his parents conflict, what does he do? The wife can help or hinder him in his dilemma, depending on what she expects of him and helps him to do.

In Western Europe too, the trend is towards more partnership in families. Once the male was the unquestioned authority of the household. When father came home, everybody behaved carefully, spoke respectfully, jumped to obey. Gradually, this master role is being replaced by a sharing of family authority by the husband and wife; even the children are frequently consulted for their opinions. Furthermore, married women in Europe are increasingly holding jobs. In France, for example, a country where women have long worked outside their homes, one out of every three married women works. In the Scandinavian countries, Italy, and Germany, the number rises steadily.

European men, who once scorned the idea, are beginning to help with the care of house and children as men of the United States have been doing since the days of the early pioneers. In Sweden, special courses in housekeeping have been offered to married men. Courses for "Expectant Fathers" are less of a joke than they once were. Domestic help is becoming scarce. Girls would rather go into industry with its regular hours, higher pay, and greater companionship than into domestic service. Balances shift within the home. This is rarely easy. "The break-up of the joint family is excellent for the woman, but it has a bad effect on youth," writes an Asian university professor. "My college students do not seem to know right from wrong. In the old days of community living, it was the duty of the grandparents to read the Hindu Scripture aloud to the children. Now no one seems to have time. . . ."[8]

Mothers, caring deeply for the happiness of their families, can do much. Husbands and children alike feel uncertain and adrift, cut off from the old ways, but not yet secure in the new. Women also feel adrift, but women are the homemakers. In all the little domestic ways they know so well, they can help their families to remain united and secure while gradually they all become accustomed to new conditions.

At the 1959 United Nations Seminar in Bogotá, Latin-American women discussed the widespread problem of bridging the gap between the generations to make the transitional period easier for both. They agreed on three ways in which women could ease the situation. They should:

> Work to establish classes for mothers in their own children's schools, so they will better understand their children's new horizons.
>
> Set up special classes in the poorer communities to help the mothers catch up with their children's advances.
>
> Arrange that mothers visit the schools more often and teachers visit the homes so that both sides understand one another better.

These are tiny steps in the right direction, aimed at crossing boundaries that divide, but the problem lies still deeper. What we all must seek are ways to help people adjust. Mothers with understanding and patience have a major contribution to make as generations rub against one another in this shifting period.

MEN

Throughout much of the world, men have long considered women to be inferior to themselves.

A plane was on its way from Dhahran to Jidda in Saudi Arabia in 1949. The pilot said that reservations had been made for six people in Riad, but when he stopped there, six men and six women came aboard. "How about these women?" he asked the leader of the group. "Oh," was the surprised answer, "do you mean we have to count them too?" In most places this male attitude towards women is changing. Men begin to want companionship as well as cooking. As they become more educated, they want educated wives with whom they can talk about daily affairs; they want to be able to take their wives with them as they travel; they want to be proud of them in the community. Fortunately it works both ways. As women are taking a more active role in the life around them, men find it easier to see them in a new light. Increasingly, the problems of our time present themselves to men and to women as a matter of shared concern.

A "mutahr" or farmer in East Europe was discussing serious business affairs with a judge. He startled the traditional old man by suddenly leaping to his feet.

"Oh, please excuse me," he said hurriedly, "I must go home. I did not know it was so late. I promised my wife to be back in time to look after the children so she can go to a meeting."

Someone asked a Caribbean woman how it was that she seemed so much more free and relaxed than were all her friends. Although like them she had several small children, she seemed to have time for more activities, be better groomed and more rested than her neighbors. She laughed and said, "Before I married I told my husband that I was used to the freedom and independence of being a single working woman. I told him that I liked that, but that I also liked him. I agreed to marry him and give up my outside work, but he agreed to let me pay myself a small housekeeping fee out of the housekeeping budget; he also agreed that I should give myself a day off every week. It works very well. I keep myself more interesting to him too. We have more to share when I am not wholly submerged by the small details of the household."

Wars and struggles for independence have broken through the tight chrysallis which once bound women in many parts of the world. Suddenly, in war, men have realized women's competence, their steadfastness, their versatility, their capacity to run a home well while at the same time doing work outside. In times of turmoil women have had the chance to show that they *could* work alongside their men in the building of a nation without losing their femininity or jeopardizing their homes.

In pleading for American women's suffrage before Congress in 1918, at the close of World War I, President Woodrow Wilson said:

> We have made partners of women in this war; shall we admit them only to a partnership of suffering and sacrifice and toil, and not to a partnership of privilege and right?

President Bourguiba had the same attitude about the women of Tunisia after that country's war for independence. Like so many others throughout the Arab world, Tunisian women had lived hidden away for centuries, veiled, considered inferior, useful merely for producing babies. Parents were disappointed in the birth of girls because they could not earn money, except what was paid to buy them in marriage, and often that was not much. From the time they were babies, the poor little girls had a hard time. If two children argued, the girl had to give in. Brothers were always right no matter what the situation. And girls were taught to be demure in front of men, to drop their eyes and withdraw from sight, even from their fathers, husbands, and brothers.

In 1934 the country started to fight for its independence. It was a hard-fought, weary struggle for freedom. At first the women were not much involved, but then they began to go into exile with their men—into prison with them, into poverty and hiding; they began to serve as messengers and to look after the wounded. Little by little they became more and more useful in the national struggle.

Then, because Tunisians are a combination of French and Arab, full of energy and vitality, women began to do more things on their own. They rioted and staged demonstrations. Thousands of them were imprisoned. During World War II, when people were fighting all over the world for various kinds of freedom, Tunisian women were among those of many nations who took an active part in underground activities.

They won male respect. Not only did they work hard and responsibly, but they shared enormous hardships without flinching.

The result was that in 1956 when their country at last became independent after seventy-five years of French rule, women were given equal rights with men. They could vote; divorce became a matter of legal decision in the courts. Men could no longer simply say "I divorce you" three times and throw a woman out into the street without means of support. This can still happen in many parts of the Arab world, and also frequently in Asia; but here, for the first time in an Arab country, Tunisian women, as well as men, had rights in marriage. A woman was recognized at last as a person with dignity. Throughout the whole Middle Eastern world Tunisian women gave evidence that men *could* change their attitudes—that women *could* gain respect.

HOW ARE MEN WON OVER?

There appear to be three stages in women's development and the sequence appears to be the same, no matter what the country:

1. *Home-Centered.* She is the ornament—or slave as the case may be—of the home. Her interest centers about children, cooking, sewing.
2. *Woman-Centered.* In the second stage women have more education, and become not only conscious of but concentrated on their own rights and status and opportunities.
3. *Equal.* The third stage—and achieved to a remarkable degree in some countries like Indonesia and Burma—is that in which women and men work side by side in jobs both big and small without regard to sex but only to merit and ability.

Some years ago a distinguished group of women delegates to the United Nations General Assembly discussed: "What are the obstacles that prevent women from taking their rightful responsibilities?"[9]

High on their list was the same, familiar answer: "Men."

"Many women do not take their proper role because they prefer to be mere 'dolls' for the men," said one delegate. "They will not stand up and fight and work as citizens."

"Women have to be two or three times as capable as men to compete with them," said others. "This is true partly because the woman in public life has two or three jobs to fill—wife, mother, career—whereas the man can concentrate his efforts on one job. Partly it is because men demand higher qualifications of women than of each other. They require them to be more mature for they have less trust in their capacities. Women have to prove themselves over a long period before they are given opportunity."

Others pointed out that women *are* taking responsibility in many fields—political, social, economic. "When more women take part in their country's political life," it was said, "when they are active enough to have a real impact on a country, men do turn to them for ideas and for their energy and abilities."

Women do not have to "demand" position once they have earned it. Not all countries understand this. In some of the newer nations, women are seeking high posts before they have qualified in the eyes of men by hard work at more modest levels. Elsewhere, women have earned men's real respect. The Civic Assembly of Women of the Philippines, for example, has a prestige which women of many nations, including the United States, can envy. The Assembly, representing 770,000 women of forty-five different groups, has a standing relation with the Philippine Government whereby it submits names for appointment to government jobs.

"We submit three names and the President takes one," said Helen Benitez, then President of the Civic Assembly. "We never recommend a woman if we do not think she is as good or better than any man available for the job."

Does she feel that Philippine women have a fair representation in government jobs? "Not yet, but their number is increasing," she answered.

The general trend throughout today's world is for men and

women to work more closely together in all fields—in the family, at work, in the community, and in politics. It has often been said that "If the country is an eagle, then women are one of the wings." This must mean that they stop thinking of themselves as separate and apart. An Australian writer put her opinion squarely on the table:

> Women must cease to tuck themselves away into well-meaning but ineffectual little organizations of their own. They must step into the existing male-dominated organizations—particularly those having a bearing on Government—and assume their fair share of responsibility in shaping the order of society. To this end they must join political parties in effective numbers. This could be done very effectively in outer urban and rural communities. Eventually they would be able to nominate and vote in sufficient strength inside the party to have a woman candidate for a worthwhile seat. As it is at present, women are nominated for hopeless electorates merely to test the market or keep the pot boiling until it is considered worth having a male candidate to carry the day.
>
> Women should rebel against being relegated to "ladies auxiliaries"—the tea or coffee-makers for male meetings and the fund raisers for the men. Most political or social organizations could not exist without their "auxiliaries." Yet rarely do the "auxiliaries" have a voice on the male-dominated executive. Why are they not in equal numbers on the main executive, and the job of fund raising—or even tea making—a combined effort? I am amazed at how many women's auxiliary members are content with their place in the shadows.[10]

The same thought is echoed in Tanganyika.

> Women's organizations are not achieving much because they are separate. When a woman learns something new and the man does not know it, it is hard for her to convince him that it is good. A man and his wife must learn things together.[11]

Putting the same thing in terms familiar to the island women of the South Pacific, Miss Tani Sisa, a Papuan leader, said:

> It is no use having a new strong hull fastened to an old badly lashed outrigger; for then, when the big waves come, the outrigger will break, the hull will be swamped, and the people on the canoe will drown.
>
> It is the same with a village; the men are the hull, the women are the outrigger. If, while the men learn to do and to understand new things, we remain ignorant and backward, then we may cause the whole village—even our whole people —to be ruined. But if we work and train ourselves, then we shall be like a strong outrigger, and our village, like the well-built canoe, will be safe, even in rough seas.[12]

There are many factors which still keep close co-operation between men and women from being universal:

1. *Attitudes.* Some men still think that women are naturally and fundamentally inferior beings.
2. *Deep Cultural Traditions.* Easy relationships in public between men and women may be prevented for quite some time in many parts of the world by old cultural customs.
3. *Time.* Men usually work during the day, while women's best free hours are during the day when children are at school and husbands at work.
4. *Shyness.* Many women, even in cultures where social mixing appears to be easy, are too shy to speak up when men are present. They sit quietly even though in their own groups they have ideas, originality, and ability.

Men and women each have their role to play. Their basic aims are the same. Both want to rid the world of the specter of war; both want a better future for themselves and for their children. If life is to be more full, if children are to grow up healthier and better educated, if cities are to be reborn without the misery of slums, then at every level and in every country men need women's help to bring about such changes. Women have a tremendous part to play in lifting levels of health, in raising standards of homes, in contributing to a nation's economic growth. There is no need for them to feel competitive, to turn "hard," to lose their femininity, or to desert their families.

They can do it softly.

Paramount Chieftainess Ella Gulama of Sierra Leone came to the United States to discuss trade, shipping, mining, tourism, and other business subjects normally considered men's work.

In her canary yellow turban and flowing robes, she endeared herself to the businessmen in New York and other cities. It was not only her charm, but her combination of skill, knowledge, and ability which won her deep respect. Prior to her departure, nearly seventy-five men gathered in New York from Detroit, Boston, and Baltimore to pay her honor at a farewell luncheon. Here Chief Ella displayed diplomacy and femininity of a kind which would assure a woman's acceptance in any male circle.

After many flowery and laudatory speeches, Chief Ella was asked, "To what do you attribute your great success here in New York?" She rose to her feet with a sweet, shy smile. "If I have had any success," she said gently, "perhaps it is because I just love *men."*

In general, men tend to support women's activities as soon as they begin to see that their wives are not neglecting them at home and that the effects are beneficial, reflected in their homes and communities. They tend to accept them in responsible posts when they see they are well qualified, but feminine and noncompetitive.

Women still have a long way to go in many areas. This was pointed up dramatically in a Plenary Resolution passed quietly by the Women's Seminar of 1962 in Kenya, East Africa. The Resolution requested: "That the beating of wives be declared illegal."[13]

Three

Education

"PLEASE WILL YOU tell us," asks a mother from one of the Indonesian Islands, "how do we prepare our children for a world we do not understand?"

No one can predict what will be the future demands on tomorrow's men and women, but for this complicated world one thing seems sure: For both men and women, education is no longer a privilege, but a necessity of modern life. It is needed for work, for citizenship, and for the fulfillment of each individual.

The desire of men for better educated, companionable wives vitally affects schooling for girls. What should girls—and boys too—be learning nowadays in order to prepare them for a space age, an age of automation, an age when, through the marvels of communication and travel, every nation becomes close neighbor to every other?

With modern technology spreading rapidly through the world, the need grows for educated intelligence rather than for pure physical strength. Through voting, the power of the individual increases. It is, therefore, vital that his understanding be broad, so that his vote may be a wise one.

At present more than 50 per cent of the population of

many countries are illiterate—more in rural areas than in cities, more women than men, more adults than young. This does not mean that these people are not intelligent; it does mean that changes in cultural traditions, ways of earning a living, ways of learning new skills are affected.

To help such vast numbers catch up with the twentieth century, teachers are needed. They need not only professional training but also a grasp of their subject, for without this one is merely spreading ignorance. How does the world acquire enough trained teachers quickly?

A recent study of one of the major African countries revealed that 73 per cent of the teachers had only primary school training. Dr. C. E. Beeby, writing of "Education in Emergent Countries"[1] says that throughout the Pacific areas, enormous classes—often over one hundred pupils—are frequently taught by untrained teachers with meager equipment. Much material throughout the world is being learned by rote, rarely understood; tables or strings of words are often chanted in unison until learned. Questions are not encouraged, because the teacher feels too insecure about the answers.

The marvel is that the thirst for learning is so strong that despite these handicaps, children *are* learning. They are completing secondary school and passing external examinations. Their potential must be tremendous. As systems under which they are learning improve, they will surge ahead.

Never before in the long human history has mankind been so determined to put every child into school. Dr. J. Roby Kidd, Director of the Social Science Research Council of Canada, speaking on "UNESCO at the Crossroads," said:

> Whatever you may feel about the difficulties and perils of today, these are marvelous times.
>
> Never before in the long history of the human species did

> men determine seriously to put every child in school, but that is now the target for 1980, and already a hundred countries have agreed to invest about 4 per cent of their gross national product in the effort; they are already planning how the 9.5 million teachers that will be needed will be found, recruited, trained, and equipped. In addition, there is in formation a campaign to reach all of the illiterate men and women in the world, those "silent ones" who, throughout the ages, have lacked the key that unlocks much of what is worthwhile in life. This is nothing more or less than an endeavour to put half a billion people in the classroom in the next ten years. Even if we are to miss by as much as 50 per cent, it will still be the most momentous and far-reaching educational and social event ever attempted, enrolling a student body of 250 million men and women.[2]

One of the vital concerns of those who plan today's education should be to see that students are not educated *away* from their own people. In order to come to better grips with reality, each nation's educated people should understand local customs, traditions, superstitions, taboos, and ancient lore that still affect their own people. One of today's silent dangers lies in the gap that is developing within countries themselves, dividing the schooled from the unschooled.

The difficult questions which face us all are: "What are the traditional elements that must carefully be retained in the face of the world's bewildering pace and, equally important, what must be thrown aside to make way for the new?"

"Education for everyone" is only a part of what needs to concern us. The *content* of what is being taught inside the schools should be of serious concern as well. Few of us seem to know clearly what our children are actually learning once they get to school. For what are they being prepared? Where does the emphasis lie? How much are children still repeating from memory? How much are they learning to think and reason, with creativity, critical ability, and flexibility of mind? The actual curriculum naturally must vary from country to country, related to the needs of each. But there are some basic lines of guidance.

Mr. George V. Allen of the United Kingdom, in addressing the World Food Congress in June 1963, said:

> It is possible to define . . . two main purposes which an educational system in any country should have. These are:
>
> 1. To instill an understanding of certain basic concepts common to all mankind. [Concepts of mathematics, chemistry, etc., apply everywhere regardless of nation or region.]
>
> 2. To promote an understanding of the cultural heritage and the social organization of each country or group, and of its relation to other countries and to the world. . . .[3]

He suggests that at the secondary level children should:

> learn something of their own history, geography, and culture and in addition to the basic principles of science, something of their own flora, fauna, and natural resources.
>
> It also is essential that the standards in the secondary schools [in the new countries] should not be lower than those in developed countries.[4]

In the United States, as elsewhere, the debate ranges about what should be included in a curriculum. How much should young people study liberal arts? How much time should go to vocational training in order to develop saleable skills in this competitive age? Do the young need social studies to fit them as "well-rounded" personalities, or is it the task of a school to concentrate on mathematics, science, language, and history? Is their task primarily to equip minds or to develop personalities? Is there enough time for the schools to undertake both?

A few years ago the country was so much agitated about what were considered serious lacks in the American educational system that a White House Conference was called to determine what the people of the nation wanted. Preparation went on all over the country for nearly two years before the Conference.

First, every tax-supported school throughout the country was invited to send representatives from both faculty and parents' organizations to attend a series of meetings held in the local communities. Far into the night, agitated citizens discussed what they felt their local schools needed to prepare their children well for today's world.

Next, each community selected its best representatives and sent them to a second series of sessions, held now at the county level. These spokesmen in turn chose representatives for a later series of state-level meetings.

On they worked until, nearly two years later, several hundred selected representatives met at the White House in Washington, ready to reflect the thinking of the people of the United States, from the great urban centers down to the smallest rural community.

Out of this meeting, which lasted several days, came specific recommendations regarding curriculum—not only its content but its stress and emphasis also: how to balance science and the arts; timing; pressures on children; discipline; college requirements; vocational guidance and training. Recommendations, stemming in this way from the people themselves, are having a widespread effect throughout the public school system of the land.

Everywhere the "wind of change" is being felt in education. The old porcelain factory at Sèvres, France, has been converted into an International Teachers' Center, known as the Centre International D'Études Pedagogique. Here teachers assemble to study and discuss the changes needed to revitalize their educational systems. For centuries the tradition of European education concentrated on a small number of carefully selected children, most of whom were going into professions. Now, when so many more children need to be educated, the system must be radically reformed. A new emphasis on science, modern languages, and the social sciences is being coupled with new ways of teaching. In September 1960, various ideas from this Center finally became law in France. Gradually they are being adopted in the schools; little by little they will influence the entire French school system.

Education for girls needs special scrutiny, partly because it is new in many parts of the world where girls have heretofore had little access to education; partly because the lives for which girls are being fitted tend to be broader nowadays than once was true. What do today's girls need to know in order to be good wives, mothers, and citizens?

Dr. Richard Glenn Gettell, President of Mount Holyoke College in Massachusetts, once made a plea "For the Uncommon Woman." In his estimation, the primary approach should be an education of the highest quality,

> consciously focused on developing the intelligent young woman's ability to learn for herself, so that whatever she chooses to do, and whenever, she has the inner resources, the curiosity, and the mental ability to face and master new challenges.[5]

Mothers talk about their children's education all over the world, especially their daughters' schooling, because they are restless and uneasy about it; they are searching, and feel unsettled from many points of view.

A Y.W.C.A. group in East Africa said:

> We worry about our girls. There are some things we wish we could change about their education. They lose all interest in the village. They never lower themselves any more. What has happened to humility?[6]

Another member of the same group:

> If we just copy, we lose our desire to take risks. We get too tamed. The young seem to copy these days. In this big continent we will fail if we copy too closely.[7]

A mother from Iran said this:

> My great concern is the uncertainty that lies ahead. I fear the moral dangers to which my children are exposed due to three things:
> 1. Decline in parental authority.
> 2. Lack of suitable recreation facilities.
> 3. Not enough reading material that is suitable.
>
> I believe our curriculum should find room to provide scope for character training and the development of leadership wherever it exists. Could not the schools do more to create a sense of national purpose and the ideal of service to one's community?[8]

In country after country, girls are responding eagerly to whatever new opportunities arise. "Open a school today and it is full tomorrow," says the Chief Inspectress of Girls' Schools in East Pakistan.

With long black pigtails flying, Pakistani girls flock to all available schools, reaching eagerly beyond their former "purdah" environment. They crowd into double sessions, as at the Jacob Line High School in Karachi which has 950 girls in one session and 700 in another, despite a great shortage of teachers and lack of equipment. This crowding occurs not only because parents are showing a new desire to educate their daughters, but also because many of the schools themselves are blossoming forth with new life, preparing girls for far greater freedom and responsibility.

The fundamental change in basic attitude within many schools is clearly demonstrated by one specific example:

In a town in East Africa in 1951, a vivid, eager young woman was sent to take over the Arab Girls School. It was housed in old Arab quarters and although 168 girls were enrolled, about seventy to seventy-five were perpetually absent. Writes the headmistress:

> The building was gloomy and surrounded by narrow streets, no graveling or even a square yard of grass. The girls left home veiled and escorted to step out into the narrow streets and shuffle to school, anything from one-half hour to an hour late. Here the bars clanged, the old door swung open a foot to admit the children and swung to, the old Duenna resuming her seat of vigilance. Inside, lessons droned on to twelve. No free play, no free thinking, in fact, no freedom. Twelve noon and the escorts queued up to remove their veiled bundles. School was over for the day.
>
> What of the girls? Or shall I say bundles? Back in their fathers' houses, they moved about in the women's quarters. What did they do? Well, they went home. Did they cook? Some did, but most had servants. . . . Did they read? No, they had no books. . . . And these were to be the women of the next generation, wives, and mothers—chattels without ambition, and yet many bright faces among them.
>
> To cut a long story short, despite struggles and opposition, we have one of the finest schools on the island, built on six acres of ground, all well developed and planned into playing fields. Very few are escorted now; they are trusted instead. Our roll stands at 669 girls, and very few absentees—32 seniors are working for Senior exams, of whom I hope six will go to University. . . .
>
> Last year we won the Junior Physical Education cup and were champion company for the Girl Guide contest in the Province. This is most encouraging, but there is much to do

> yet. Over 700 girls remain who are getting no education whatever, and my thoughts are always with them. They will come yet, but the tide is slow. How will I get them? . . . Well, at a wedding I will meet the mother or the sister or "the rest of the family," be invited in, see four or five unfamiliar little faces in the women's quarters and then, persuasion. They come, but only four of the five, and that means another visit, and so on.
>
> I think my greatest feeling of confidence came when 20 Girl Guides from the Company that I had such a struggle to start came to camp 260 miles away, at the edge of the forest belt. Veils were stored away on arrival and a happier, freer lot of children you never met. . . . Think of it; five years only had elapsed since we had closed the doors of our slum building . . . but there I was alone, the only adult, and all my assistants were our own Guides, running the camp by themselves, and doing it extraordinarily well.[9]

Women can help the process of change by welcoming and seeking new ideas regarding their children's schooling. This may mean asking leading questions of the local Education Board; it may mean visiting the school to search out exactly what is being taught and how; it may mean attending meetings of local authorities to support or protest their decisions; it may mean stirring citizens' clubs and organizations to action towards changing some laws.

Since one of the world's great shortages is that of teachers, imaginative thought is needed regarding both the creation of more teachers and efficient use of those who exist.

The Minister of Elementary Education in Taiwan observed:

> In one single building we have 10,000 children. We have a total of two million children of elementary age in Taiwan. This means that one teacher will have as many as 60-70 children in each class, or some 350 or more papers to correct every night! You can imagine how hard it is to know how each individual child is getting on.[10]

In the United States, as elsewhere, the teacher shortage is acute. Many families are concerned because their children are being poorly taught in overcrowded classrooms. Parents are trying to ease the situation by offering their own free hours on a voluntary basis, to relieve teachers of some of that routine work which does not require a professional background. Parents correct papers, run libraries, read aloud, type, and keep records. They can help in this way to ease the critical shortage by giving skilled teachers more time for their tasks. Perhaps this could be done in more countries.

As time goes on, more will doubtless be done with films, radio, and television to supply teaching to hundreds of children who otherwise could not be in school at all, or only under inferior teachers. These media are being extended as aids to learning in many places, and adapted to local needs. They can never take the place of teachers, but they can bring outstanding lecturers to thousands of people and thus extend and expand their experience. There are admittedly handicaps and difficulties in the teaching use of outside aids but clearly the old traditional classroom methods are becoming less and less adequate to handle the demands being made on overcrowded classrooms in this urgent age.

Many countries are using mass media for teaching:

In France: Teleclubs encourage group viewing of agricultural programs, followed by group discussions.

In Italy: Telescuola provides teaching for children who have no school within their own area.

In Canada: the national radio program has a vast rural adult education program, reaching the whole way across from sea to sea.

In the Andes of Colombia: Throughout the jagged

mountains where Colombia, Peru, and Ecuador meet, everyone knows the name of Father Salcedo, a Roman Catholic priest who came there to live many years ago.

The poverty of the gullied mountain farms depressed and concerned him when he arrived, as did the boredom and poor health of his parishioners. He worried about additional souls living in remote valleys who were not in anyone's care.

Starting with a homemade transmitter and three small receivers, Father Salcedo has built a "Radio School of the Air" through the years, which now reaches over many miles. Using the air waves, he has been able to teach his people about contour ploughing and fertilizers; about child care and nutrition; about music and reading. Eyes are brighter; life has new interest for hundreds in those remote valleys; there is a new vigor of spirit. Farms are prospering and gullies are now rare. The priest's work has proven so successful that an agreement has been put into effect between the Colombian Government and the United Nations. The U.N. has agreed to support Father Salcedo in his one-man effort to raise standards of life for the poor *campesinos* of the mountains.

From Sudan to South Africa the airways chatter at appointed hours with talks and classes, hints, and household advice in many vernaculars and dialects, carrying new knowledge deep into countless compounds and huts and villages. These are "Magazines of the Air," special weekly programs designed to help Africa's women adapt themselves quickly to new conditions.

Writes Miss Isla Bunbury in *African Women:*

The enemies of listening . . . are lack of primary education, lack of interest [because of fatigue] produced by hard physical work and habitual lack of time for listening. Broadcasts for women have to be fitted into the woman's day, particularly the rural woman's day. . . . [It is likely she] must go out of the house for community listening at some school, coffee shop or other meeting place. It must be worth her while to make the effort.

Then she is not trained to listen attentively for any length of time, especially to a disembodied voice. Therefore the talks must be of short duration. . . . The housewife . . . hates to be talked at. Often she sees no point at all in listening to advice: she thinks she knows better or that experiments . . . will not find favour with her husband.

In general, broadcasting in Africa has to be on a very personal level. There must evolve a personal relationship. Auntie Grace is someone you know, to whom you can write and who will answer your questions. . . . You come to share her problems, you know how many children she has . . . and what she herself cooks. The African woman must be able to identify herself with the broadcaster. . . .[11]

Women can help to improve the quality of broadcasts by mobilizing the expression of public opinion in favor of good programs. Stations are sensitive to the desires of their public. Says Mr. George V. Allen of Great Britain:

It is to be hoped that [stations in developing countries] will not follow the lead [of trivia] set by some of the sophisticated countries, but will present to populations hungry for information programs on subjects of significance and importance to them.[12]

Women can help extend the availability of radio to more people in various ways. They can raise money to send small receivers to "Listening Posts" in remote areas. They can support the best programs that are already being provided, calling public attention to them in advance, asking for rebroadcasts, using the tapes and records later in their own meetings.

House-to-house surveys done in their own localities, after consultation with the broadcasting companies, would help to find out answers to such questions as:

Are the present programs understood?
What misunderstandings occur?
What items are hard for listeners to grasp?
Are the hours convenient?
What type of programs do listeners wish stations would carry?

Women can help broadcasters and program planners to determine what the public likes and wants.

The more the media realize the full extent of their role, the better they can fill it. Radio can help transcend the shortage of teachers or the difficulty of transport; it can offer education to women in their homes, thereby helping them to keep up with their husbands and children; it can bring new ideas to those far removed from the cities.

Education is, of course, far more than a child's physical presence for a few years in a school building. It is the basis of citizenship, of economic ability, of a nation's health; it is the preservation of the best of an old heritage while being alert to grasp the best of a new. It no longer means learning by rote. It means developing initiative and originality of thought; encouraging creativity and flexibility; strengthening those qualities which lead to world citizenship—as well as imparting facts.

Women, in whose hands lies the responsibility for the next generation, must see that their children are taught to keep pace with these fast-moving times. Furthermore, they must seize their own opportunities to read and listen and learn, so that they will not be cut off from the next generation by lack of comprehension. In addition, all of us have a personal responsibility to take some part in reducing the appalling illiteracy that still holds millions of adults in ignorance, cut off from access to the world's thought.

"Each one teach one" is an old familiar saying throughout the world. But how much has each one of us given in time, care, and compassion to make this a reality? How many of us have *actually* taught one other person—a servant, a driver, a janitor, the workman in a factory, or, perhaps, someone coming from another land who is struggling to learn our language? What a power it would be throughout the world if indeed each person took seriously the slogan: "Each one teach one!"

Four

The Vote and Public Office

> It is in [politics] that issues vital to our existence are being solved. In my view, every woman must concern herself with politics—and by politics I do not just mean voting; I mean involving oneself in the life of the nation and the world. Politics is no longer a pastime. It is life and death, and there can be no sidestepping of our responsibility except at peril to everything we profess to believe in.[1]

So SPOKE Madame Pandit of India. Decisions made by politicians reach into every home, affect every woman and all of her family, whether she realizes it or not.

It has only been within the last seventy-five years that women have voted. First in Finland, then in New Zealand and years later in Australia, then in Norway and Canada men have gradually given women the privilege of voting in elections. In the United States, women's struggle for the franchise went on for seventy long years before it was finally achieved—as recently as 1921.

Now, women in all but nine countries have the vote (and in some of these nine, the men do not vote either). Some women have fought for it; it has been granted to others without effort on their part. Some value it deeply, but many do not as yet realize that with the privilege of taking part in government there is also a responsibility. Some think achieving women's "rights" means that they should immediately be granted official posts, whether or not they are prepared for them. Others use their vote without truly understanding either its power or the facts on which they are expressing their voice. Too many do not use their ballot at all.

Patience J. Hamilton of Sierra Leone writes:

> I suggest we start early through schools, colleges, clubs and societies. Every girl or woman should be taught to know her rights and privileges, and also her responsibilities.
>
> Women should be helped to vote wisely by means of mock elections, radio debates (in the vernacular), films, balloting, and talks on local and world affairs. They should also be advised about the danger of voting for friends, or of being swayed merely by appearance or wealth. Through their organizations women can help each other by encouraging as many as possible to take part in conferences, by organizing discussions, and by putting forth information about other countries and people.[2]

Women cannot sit back with the comfortable feeling "My place is in the home; I have nothing to do with politics." Decisions such as conscription, condemnation of property, changes in employment opportunities, taxation rates, and similar issues are of grave importance to them as well as to men. A whole way of life can be altered by the decision of a political body.

This is why it is important for women to understand their responsibilities and to prepare themselves so that they can play an increasingly useful role in local and national politics.

Legally speaking, the whole theory of democracy is founded on representation of the people—of all the people—by those who are elected. A genuine free ballot is the keystone of free government. It is no wonder, therefore, that far-sighted women have long been demanding the right to vote and the right to be represented in forming national policy. Women have a great contribution to make to society: "He who wears the shoe knows where it pinches." Women know where many needs lie. Their experience, their compassion, and their insight give them not only the right to speak but also the obligation.

Political parties now are conscious that they need women's votes. There is therefore a greater effort to consider their problems and thus to win their support. Women's vote can still be easily exploited because, in general, most women are inexperienced; many are indifferent. As a result, politicians work hard—by fair means and foul—to gain their support. In many countries women's organizations realize that they face a new challenge to educate not only the illiterate but also those of all classes who are still politically naive or uninformed.

"The only thing necessary for a triumph of evil," it has been said, "is for good men to do nothing." Far too often voters "do nothing." Bad laws are passed, or poor leaders chosen, because people did not care enough to cast their ballot on the side of good. In many countries, the League of Women Voters and kindred groups are struggling to explain both sides of issues impartially, to warn against pressures, to get voters to the polls, to guard against bribery or undue influence.

There is a need for more women to unite objectively on common problems, examining the pros and cons of issues without being emotional about them. This is not easy, especially for those who are used only to domestic problems which are so often both emotional and personal. Bigger issues require a bigger viewpoint, without the element of self.

At the first Women's Seminar in Kenya Miss Doro recommended:

> Once you have voted and the candidate takes office, what do you do then? You keep an eye on your public officials. How many of you know whether your elected representative took his place with the Opposition in Legislative Council yesterday. Did you approve? . . . I can tell you a bit about what American women have done. They have organized themselves into groups in order to strengthen their views, to inform the public and to impress on legislators their ideas as to what the community needs, by campaigns of letter-writing and signing of petitions. For example, the Parent-Teachers Association is concerned with the problems of education, proper environ-

ments for schoolchildren, maintaining high standards and obtaining qualified teachers. . . . They influence school boards and state agencies which deal with legislation regarding education.

There are other groups that take interest in their communities. Some are concerned with health problems, others with working conditions. But all do two things, which you can easily do:

1. They gather facts and attempt to inform the public in order to enlighten the electorate. . . .
2. They speak with one voice for those things which are important to them.

Women, at least those whose prime concern is the future of their families, find it easy to work together because they have a common goal. So they are willing to work as volunteers. If human beings in one part of the world can do this, then human beings elsewhere can also organize themselves.

She urged:

1. Survey your needs.
2. Decide the order in which you can meet these needs.
3. Inform yourselves on what is being done now and what can be done in the future.
4. Use your vote intelligently.
5. Speak with a united voice to government and its agencies.[3]

Countries do not generally record the women's vote separately from the men's; therefore it is difficult to get figures on how much women actually use their vote. Studies have been made, however, that indicate:

Fewer women go to the polls than men.
The difference [in number of men and women voting] is smaller than you might suppose.
The gap is narrowing as women learn more about the issues and how to use their franchise.[4]

Bayan Fitma Saltung, former President of the Izmir Republican Women's Association in Turkey, emphasized the growing interest that women, and especially the less educated, were showing in the vote in her country. Eighty per cent of the women vote in the village election, she said, even though men often try to discourage them.

"Women turned the tide in the vote between the Protectorate and the Colony," said a West African from Sierra Leone. "We thought we knew about how the election would turn out, but we did not reckon with the long lines of women that turned out in quiet, patient queues to vote for the up-country point of view. There were thousands of them, and they all came."[5]

On the whole, differences between the votes of men and women are slight, with women somewhat favoring the conservative and religious parties. At first, therefore, one might think the influence of women on election results was negligible, but one must not forget two points:

1. Politicians now have to keep women's interests in their minds.
2. There is an unmeasurable ("indirect") influence of wives over husbands, as well as of husbands over wives.

Although the proportion of women taking part in political life through the ballot is only slightly smaller than that of men (and in some areas, such as in West Africa, it may be larger), the same is not true when you look at how many actually hold office in parliaments, local assemblies, or municipal governments. Rarely do women hold higher than five per cent of the seats in a parliament, except in the U.S.S.R., where it is reported that seventeen per cent of the members of the Supreme Soviet are women. In traditionally "feminist" countries, the situation is as bad or worse than in countries where women have heretofore been kept in relative seclusion. In the United States, for example, only two per cent of the members of Congress are women.

An Australian writes:

> Here in the third country of the world to grant the franchise to women, we are still not eligible in all states for jury service; there are no women judges; no women are admitted to the highest grade of public service, the administrative division; in many professions and employments we do not receive equal pay for equal work.[6]

"Although we have had the vote since 1952," observes a Lebanese woman, "there are still no women members of Parliament. This is due to male antagonism, for the majority of our men still consider women to be their intellectual inferiors."[7]

Marjorie Tait, considering why so few women are in political positions anywhere, wrote:

> Hitherto in most parts of the world women have led lives which brought them into far less contact with public affairs than men and this is true even where most men have had little political power. Yet the lives of women have been influenced equally with those of men by government policies: war or peace, agricultural reform, industrialization, foreign trade, all touch women too. Can we make women see how they live in a great web which shakes when it is touched at any point?[8]

Women's own attitude toward themselves is perhaps the most important key to their position. These attitudes were revealed to some extent in a series of essays submitted in a world-wide competition held by the Committee of Correspondence in 1960. From many countries it was reported frankly that women tend to be passive rather than active; "resigned rather than rebellious." Essay after essay spoke of women's "apathy, sense of inferiority, willingness to 'let someone else do it' ":

> Women are unsure of themselves and their opinions; they must first be shown the problems before they can even think about the solutions.
>
> In my country—Italy—women feel no sense of responsibility towards the community.
>
> Our Finnish women still struggle with their traditional feelings of insecurity and incompetence.[9]

Almost everywhere, relatively few women are listed as candidates for public office. Many women think this is due to deliberate discrimination on the part of men, who frequently opposed women's suffrage in the first place. Men lead the political parties and influence the choice of candidates. Men, on the other hand, say, "There is a shortage of well-qualified women to run for office; furthermore, the public, including women themselves, do not vote for women, so we cannot put them up."

Moreover, when women *are* in the political arena, they are seldom in key areas. Their work in parliaments, in legislative assemblies, in congresses, and even in the United Nations, is generally concerned with health, welfare, children's problems, and women's rights, rather than with problems of disarmament, budgets, political policy, or international issues.

However, this, too, is changing. One thinks of Mrs. Agda Rössel, longtime head of the Swedish Permanent Mission to the United Nations and now Ambassador to Yugoslavia; of

Mrs. Lakshmi Menon, Minister of State for External Affairs for India; of Mrs. Golda Meir, Foreign Minister of Israel; and of Mrs. Alva Myrdal, who served on the important Disarmament Commission in Geneva. One thinks of the number of women ambassadors from varied countries: Miss Frances Willis, of the United States; Mrs. Leivo-Larsson of Finland; Begum Liaquat Ali Khan and Begum Ikramullah of Pakistan; and Mrs. Trinidad LaGarda of the Philippines.

Although these key women—and others like them—may be breaking the way for more to follow, the process is not rapid. At local levels, where they might be training, few women yet hold posts of top responsibility. There are still few women mayors, burgomasters, heads of municipal councils, or members of local administrative councils. It would look as though the laws establishing the civic equality of men and women are in advance of society itself. The well-known American lawyer, Clarence Darrow, once said, "Laws should be like clothes. They should be made to fit the people they are meant to serve."

But perhaps there are occasions when laws—like clothes—are made a little bigger than is needed to allow for growth.

Women have a particular contribution to make in the area of harmonizing differences—whether these be political, racial, class, educational, or other. A high government official of Iran said some years ago:

> Women are a force for stability; not politically self-seeking, eager for social advance and for national security. Their participation in political life would be an advantage. . . .[10]

Prime Minister Balewa of Nigeria once remarked that in a country like his where there are great traditional tribal rivalries, women could play a badly needed role in helping to unify the nation:

> Men cannot resist politics. This means power-seeking, rivalry, disharmony. But women share common interests that have no concern with politics—better babies, better schools, better opportunities for earning money. Wives of rival politicians can be quite friendly together while their husbands would not sit in the same room with each other.
>
> We need women to work across tribal and regional barriers. We must do everything to help these barriers be erased. Any work along these lines would be a great contribution for Nigeria.[11]

In the world's concern over racial, religious, and tribal disturbances, the hampering effects of class barriers are often overlooked. One sees these effects in the outlawed but still existent caste system of India, in the economic hierarchies of South America, in the social distinctions of England, or in the fixed levels of "respect" in Japan and Korea. The Arabs put their feelings of rank in a proverb: "The camel has his concerns and the camel driver has his."

Women are often among the worst offenders in judging a person by status or income or position, rather than by real merit or character. But there is no class monopoly on imagination, initiative, ability, or intelligence. There is tremendous wastage for a country if talented people cannot develop to their fullest capacities, no matter how humble their origin. No resource of human skill should be wasted for a matter of class pride.

Women are in a good position to help in this regard. What can they do? Setting up contests, awards, or festivals that uncover ability in all levels of society is one means of working on the problem. Women can work to establish scholarships for schools or seminars, stating that these must be open to all, regardless of rank; they can be sure that people of different classes and groups have a chance to contribute in all kinds of conferences and planning sessions; they can themselves work closely, without regard to differences, among peoples in churches or civic groups.

Women may not yet hold many public posts, but they are becoming nationally alive. Their suffrage has definitely not been wasted. Already it has had tremendous impact, forcing people to examine habit and tradition under a strong new light; helping millions of women, through their votes, to free themselves from binding customs. Perhaps most important of all, it has made plain to all that more must be done to educate girls. Now that they vote on an equal basis with men, it is clear that girls' minds and understanding must also be developed. Increasingly, women will be able to influence the climate of public opinion; suddenly, through the sheer weight of their numbers, they have become important to the politicians.

This opens exciting new possibilities to women. What many still need to learn is how to co-ordinate their activities; how to work more closely together for the progress they desire; how to educate themselves thoroughly and impartially on the facts of an issue; how to identify themselves with other people's problems even when they do not personally share them.

The most important struggle still facing women before they take full responsibility beside men in the political arena lies within themselves. Women are still fettered by a world-wide and deep-rooted belief in their own natural inferiority. They have been taught since they were babies that this was true; their mothers believed it; their brothers and fathers and husbands believed it. But in actual fact, there is no more an inferior sex than there are inferior races. With education and opportunity, women have proven over and over again that they are the intellectual equals of men.

Women's role, first as voters, then as political figures, is extremely new in history. The wonder lies not in the fact that women have been slow to take responsible positions in their nation's life; the wonder is that so many have done so well in so brief a time.

Five

Life in the Community

A NIGERIAN WOMAN with a gentle voice made this comment:

> Once our position was simple. We were to produce children for our husbands and care for them. Now we begin to see that there is more. We watch other women play a part in the whole of life. We begin to think we women are free people, too—free to help our country. We do not want to stay any longer just grinding meal and hoeing in the fields.[1]

A young woman from the Far East sighs, "Sometimes I feel almost dizzy thinking how far we must go and how hard we must work."[2]

Most women doubtless sympathize with both points of view. For, from whatever culture they may come, women live many lives. Many see exciting new horizons in front of them but at the same time life is already full. For it can be said of woman that she is:

First of all, a wife and mother.
Often also, a contributor to family income.
A voting citizen, expected to have awareness of the issues of her community and nation.
In large measure, the transmitter of her nation's cultural heritage and traditions, for who else keeps alive the songs, stories, dances, and designs of earlier years?

In addition to all this, more and more women are making time to extend their family concern into the community so that it can become a better place in which to live.

Most women rightly think of their contribution not in terms of legislative assemblies and high political office, but rather in terms of their own families and their own neighborhoods.

"Dip your bucket where you belong and build there," says a West Indian proverb.

Despite a life which is often filled with extremely heavy labor, women are somehow finding time for such "building." In thousands of clubs, forming all over the world, women are learning new methods of feeding their children; they are listening to debates; they are learning to read. Increasing numbers of them are voting.

Women are realizing the truth of the familiar saying, "Home is your center but not your circumference." Often they move out into the community in a simple and practical manner.

Hunger and poverty are prevalent in Mexico. Señora Callignon, a distinguished Mexican lady, worried about both problems a great deal. She had no money to give, but she could not rest until she had done something to help feed her people and send their children to school.

She hit upon an idea which she took to the local branch of the Catholic Women's Society. They thought about it and discussed it, then, following a map, the members set about explaining it to each of the local families, one by one. The idea spread far and wide.

At the birth of every baby the parents would plant a slip from a pecan tree—a fast-growing and heavy-bearing nut tree of Mexico. The Catholic Women would provide the shoot. By the time the child was about ten, the tree would be bearing copiously enough for the crop to be sold, thus bringing in money for school bills. At the same time, protein would be added to the local diet.

Where possible, they urged that the child be made responsible from an early age for "his" tree so as to help him realize, while young, the value of planning ahead and working for the future.

As yet, not enough time has passed to know the results of the campaign, but so far some nine thousand trees have been planted.

Señora Callignon is waiting till both trees and babies grow but already she has wakened awareness and a desire for change.

A small rural village in Japan offers another example of how women can work in their own neighborhoods to make life better.[3]

The villagers were suffering from malnutrition; their eyes were red and watering and sore from eye infections caused by the smoke that forever filled their chimneyless homes. Their water was impure, so they were often ill.

Conditions had been like this for generations. It had not occurred to anyone that they might improve matters until one day Mrs. Matsuoka, a rural development advisor, came there.

"Tokorode," she said, "why don't we dig a new well?" Armed with pick and shovel, she and the village women went to work. They dug a new well. Then, encouraged by this success, and helped by Mrs. Matsuoka, they designed a stove with a flue. Their eyes began to feel better. They chipped in with what little money they could, and bought a pair of goats which, in due time, began to multiply. More and more of the villagers were gradually able to add goat's milk to their children's scanty diet.

Some of the major problems that women are tackling quietly in their own localities are:

Low levels of nutrition and health.

Rapid population explosion, with its destructive effects on standards of education and living.

Growth of cities with the familiar crowding, poverty, loneliness, and delinquency.

NUTRITION AND HEALTH

Who else but women can really change the feeding habits of a nation?

Scientists have been working in laboratories for years on the question of high child mortality. In Guatemala fifty of every one thousand babies in one area were dying between the ages of one and four, because mothers were weaning them before they were eighteen months old to make way for the next arrival. Once weaned, the babies were fed on starchy pap and a few vegetables, for their mothers thought they were not ready for "man's food" like eggs and meat. Such foods were, in any case, in short supply. Lacking almost all protein, the babies were ill and dying.

Now the laboratories have developed a neutral-tasting powder made from a combination of vegetable foods which grow locally. The powder makes a gruellike drink, similar to the *atole* which is familiar to them. It is almost pure protein, and since it costs only one cent a glass, it seems destined to rescue millions of protein-starved people through South and Central America.[4]

Similar low-cost vegetable mixtures are being developed from cereal combinations available in other parts of the world. One is under experimentation in Indonesia; another appears to be gaining success in Africa.

Now *whether mothers feed these powders to their families or not* is the all-important question.

Women have power in their hands to help or to hinder once scientists have opened possibilities for better nutrition.

HEALTH

In health also, mothers hold a key position, since they are entrusted with the care of growing children. Besides the individual tragedies of handicapped children, there is another aspect to the problem. Nations cannot afford to support and look after hundreds of thousands of crippled, blind, defective citizens; furthermore, countries need the capacity for work that healthy young people bring. Educated mothers can prevent—or at least diminish—much of the world's disease. For example, the eyesight of *five hundred million* people—one-sixth of the world's population—is threatened, according to the World Health Organization.[5] Many of these people, if not already blind, soon will be condemned to a life of stumbling and lonely darkness. The ghastly figures of 80 to 90 per cent of the entire rural populations of Egypt, Kuwait, Tunisia, and Libya have damaged sight. Yet, in a great number of these cases, the diseases either could have been prevented or sight could have been saved with earlier treatment if the mother had known about cleanliness and care; had been aware of the dangers of flies and dirt.

A BABY EVERY SECOND

Another basic challenge in which women are particularly concerned is the rate at which we are doubling and redoubling our population in many places. According to a United Nations study,[6] by 1970, the population of the earth will be increased by over five hundred million. Most of this increase can be expected to occur in the underdeveloped, food-short regions of Asia, Africa, and Latin America, where population growth rates in some countries are now higher than any that have been known in the history of the human race.

Millions of children all over the world are making today's shortages more and more pressingly acute. Today these children need food, clothes, medicine, schools, and teachers; tomorrow, as adults, they will need jobs, houses, land, roads, hospitals, advanced schools.

Population is actually *doubling* in many parts of the world. This is happening partly because more babies are being born; partly because people are living longer as a result of better health conditions.

In the United States and some other countries, girls are marrying so young that they have had their last baby by the time they are thirty. This speed-up of the cycle of generations can be upsetting to the emotional, as well as the economic, stability of the family.

Says Ritchie Calder in his book, *Common Sense About a Starving World:*

> Everyone, everywhere, must be brought to recognize that [the rise in population], together with the menace of nuclear destruction, is one of the two most pressing problems of our times. . . .[7]

By 1971, the population of the world will have been increased by *more people than now live in all North, South, and Central America combined.* One new soul comes into the world with every tick of the clock, day in and day out.

Most people seldom give this matter of population growth a great deal of thought, yet it has immense impact on all that is done towards peace, human dignity, and standards of decent living. It can cancel out progress; despite incredible efforts to provide teachers, for example, some countries are growing even *more* illiterate, because they cannot keep up with the new crop of children who are eager for more schooling than can be supplied.

A village girl beside Egypt's Nile expressed her awareness of the urgency:

> The old saying used to be "Every child comes into the world provided by God with all that he needs." Now we say instead: "Every child who comes into the world eats the provision of his brother." [8]

A Malaysian group stressed:

> The wanted child is the happy child, but these who are unwanted are a source of worry and deep concern. The point that people must understand is the responsibilities of parenthood. The need is to have only those children for whom provision can be made without harming those already born.[9]

Efforts are being made to assist those who want help with the problem. The United Nations has agreed to give help in family planning to any government desiring and requesting it. Several countries, notably Japan, India, Pakistan, and Egypt, are taking the family planning problem seriously and are embarking on effective action, through education and medical care. Individuals and organizations are also working hard at both national and international levels.

Mrs. Aziza Hussein, of the United Arab Republic, shows in her work how the problem moves from the community to high levels.

> I was working with a few other women to help establish one small nursery school in one of our poorest villages outside of Cairo. Naturally I came face to face with the problem of

family planning, for what help is it to a poor weary woman to provide care for one child if she is immediately tied down again with another baby and can never get her head above water?

So, I worked and talked and agitated among our leaders concerning family planning. The next year they sent me to represent the U.A.R. at the World Meeting on the subject in Singapore. There I learned more about its global implications and urgencies.

Therefore, when I found myself at the United Nations as a representative on the Commission on the Status of Women, I naturally brought this vital subject up for consideration by the twenty-one countries represented.

But that is not all. When I mentioned this later to the leaders of the International Planned Parenthood Federation, they took the matter back to the individual countries in a new way. They made contact with their committees in forty-nine nations where there are national branches of the International Council of Women. These women were soon to meet at their own world conference in Washington, D.C.

"Contact the women who will be delegates from your country," the branches were urged. "Explain the problem and its world consequences. Try to enlist them on the side of Family Planning so they will support the Resolution when it comes before their International Conference." [10]

Women went to Washington from many countries prepared to work on this vital question. The Resolution that they hammered out and passed was as follows:

Whereas, the rate of growth of the world population threatens in many countries to increase human tragedy and suffering alarmingly in the very near future—

Whereas, intensive studies by research scientists have been and are being made on human fertility, and there now exist medically approved ways to space children which are acceptable to all cultures and all religions—

Now therefore, the International Council of Women recommends:

a. That a program of education be encouraged concerning the medical, ethical and moral aspects and the dangers of the world population increase

b. That parents be educated in their duty and responsibility to plan their families in such a manner as to meet the requirements of their children

c. That, wherever possible, child-spacing information should be made available to all parents as part of the regular medical services to the community. . . .[11]

When a resolution has been approved at an international congress of any voluntary body which is accredited to the United Nations, then that group's representative may take a positive position at the United Nations. This puts the weight of thousands—often millions—of citizens behind the issue under discussion. As more and more organizations agree on a mode of action, the pressure of world opinion can become very strong.

Population growth is an area in which women's voices can be heard loudly and clearly. The impact would be strongly felt if women's organizations from all over the world spoke firmly on this matter in the councils of the world. Unless populations are stabilized in many countries, meager subsistence levels will grow rapidly worse—they are already far too low as millions of ragged, ill, and hungry people now jostle for space in the congested alleys of the world's cities.

CITIES

Yet these cities seem to have an irresistible pull, drawing people from mountains and farms where living is hard and recompense small. They seek employment, lights, companionship, and activity, moved always by the hope that "something better will turn up."

Jobs are not the only attraction. In cities where the poor are massed, there are more social benefits for the unemployed and underprivileged than exist in rural areas. In cities this is a political necessity. There are also more schools.

The growth is frighteningly rapid. Tokyo, the world's largest city, is now home for eleven million people. Buenos Aires, with 6.5 million, now has almost the same number of people as lived in the whole of Argentina as recently as 1914. There are about thirty million more Americans today than there were ten years ago. A high percentage of them are city dwellers.

When cities grow so fast, they grow without planning. Shacks and shanties spring up round the edges. There are not enough hospitals, schools, sanitary facilities; not enough food, or jobs, or places for children to play. In other words, slums sprawl over more and more miles. Slums disfigure cities; far more important, they disfigure the souls and spirits of those who inhabit them. The silent, lost people of the world's cities, whether they be in the adobe, pole, and rod huts of Mexico City, the crowded tenements of Harlem, or the tar-paper shanties of Hong Kong, long for better lives as they carry out their low-paid, menial tasks. Most of them are passive as yet. Occasionally they take part in unorganized street riots; sometimes they sit in smoke-filled rooms planning revolutionary action, but mostly they just exist, easy bait for demagogues, whether these be reactionary or leftist, Black Muslim, Communist, or agitators from some local party or persuasion.

One challenge of our time, and one in which women can play a very real part, lies in the better handling of human problems in the dark parts of our cities. Lady Bountiful will not do. Whatever efforts are made must give new spirit to the people themselves. These men and women must see how they can move out from their misery—not merely be given temporary relief measures. They need means for education, for getting better jobs, for lifting themselves and their children on a permanent basis from the squalor that surrounds them.

What can women do? Many shining individuals have shown what kind of steps are possible.

In Brazil, where illiteracy and poverty are serious problems, Dona Lenira Fraccaroli worked tirelessly to help develop children's libraries, not only as places where they could obtain books but as centers where they could feel that they belonged.

In 1936, due in large measure to her efforts, Biblioteca Infantil opened its doors in São Paulo, Brazil, with a small building and a small array of books. Ten years later, 35,000 children were registered, able to choose from 30,000 books.

The library has a modern two-story building of its own, with a Children's Theater attached. Concerts are held—folklore and classical; children come to paint, learn puppetry, publish their own newspapers, produce their own plays. There are film showings. Regularly each week the city's blind children are gathered up by buses and brought to the center where they pore over books in Braille. The library is vibrant and alive; the young flock to it.[12]

In many parts of the world, children are running away increasingly from the villages—drifting into towns with all their temptations. City children of employed—and also unemployed—mothers wander about aimlessly, frequently getting into trouble ranging from petty pilfering to organized gangs.

The Housewives Association of Norway has tackled this problem of juvenile restlessness.

> Sven is in trouble again. He doesn't like to come home after school and I hardly blame him. Grandfather complains all the time; the baby is teething and fussy; the twins have their toys all over the floor; Greta has to keep practicing her typewriting, and I am trying to cook supper. What is a twelve-year-old boy to do in two rooms? But he gets into trouble when he wanders in the streets.[13]

The Housewives Association could see that this was a major problem, not only for Sven but for hundreds of city children; they also realized that they could do something about it. They raised money and opened first one, then more, "Children's Working Rooms." After school, tumbling in with eager clatter, come both boys and girls from seven to fourteen years old. They choose what they want to do from among such useful activities as book-binding, shoemaking, carpentry, and sewing.

Led by Mrs. Engelhardt, the Housewives Association went further, for they could see that the need extended beyond merely an outlet for the children's energy. Suppose a mother were taken ill? What would happen to the family?

Working closely with the government for funds and support, the group set about training a corps of "Housewives Relief." This offers a plan of great value to many families:

Mrs. Hoftsberg, mother of four tiny children, was hit by a truck. She was rushed to the hospital. The pain of the accident was nothing compared to her anguish of spirit about her children. "I cannot go," she protested, "they will be all alone."

The muscles of her face relaxed when she was reminded that a trained "relief" would be sent by the city to live in her house and keep things running smoothly at home as long as she had to be away.

Seventeen hundred "reliefs" are now on call all over Norway, paid by the townships if the family cannot afford them. These young women study for five months before they can be appointed, learning in both theory and practice such subjects as household management, child care, and home nursing.

"Mummy," said small Lars when Mrs. Hoftsberg finally returned in her wheelchair. "When I am big I shall marry a 'Relief.' They know everything."

Libraries, play centers, children's theaters, athletic and other competitions, organized trips, glee clubs, and orchestras are healthy, creative activities that can help to stop delinquency before it starts, for delinquency is generally the result of boredom.

A sense of "belonging" is important for adults, too. They need to feel that people care; rural people suddenly transplanted to cities often feel quite desperate. They do not see any place for themselves. They can no longer cultivate the soil. Buying food with money is strange to those who are accustomed to bartering or to growing their own. Traditional educations fail in a setting where reading is essential, or where language is different. Adults as well as children need to be made to feel welcome, helped to learn skills through which they can earn; they may need help with language, or with housing problems. Women's organizations in many cities could do more than now is being done to ease the lot of those who live frightened and confused in their midst. Some may want to organize Housewives Relief, as in Norway; others might provide simple meeting places where newcomers could come together, to be treated like human beings and to share their problems with sympathetic colleagues, rather than remaining in the loneliness and anonymity of their own shacks or shanties or small hotel rooms.

Another aspect of community life belongs almost exclusively to women. If they do not take the initiative to change conditions no one else is likely to do so; I am speaking of the monotony of repetitive household labor.

For generations women everywhere have done the same heavy tasks for their homes and families—heavy scrubbing, back-breaking laundry, exhausting carrying of water or grinding of grain. These necessary tasks done over and over again, day after weary day, lead to boredom and exhaustion. No one can be creative when tired to the aching point.

Until women are freed from unimaginative duties which take hours out of every day, they will never live and contribute at their most effective levels. Mechanical and electric devices are beginning to ease the load increasingly for those who can afford them, but many throughout the world cannot pay the price, even if such equipment is available.

Nonetheless, some women are making great strides in freeing themselves and each other from monotony.

A woman in Austria first conceived of Homemaker Houses, for example. To these centers women of surrounding villages bring their laundry where they can wash it in co-operatively owned machines; they bring their fruits and vegetables to freezing units which are available for a small hourly rental, so that instead of standing alone at home for long hot hours of canning, they can freeze and preserve their family's food among their friends, in a sociable setting, using modern equipment.

In Hong Kong, systems have been established so that women share their baking, taking turns doing it for each other, so that each person does not have to spend the fuel, and the time—nor endure the boredom—of doing it herself every single day.

Many families in communities all over the world have worked out similar systems for the care of their children. Five or six congenial neighbors will develop a "baby-sitting" pool. Each afternoon of the week, one mother is "on duty." The others may leave their children to play with hers and thus have a few hours free for themselves, knowing their children have companionship and care.

Women are imaginative. Many have devised short-cuts around the house by which they save themselves time. These ideas can be shared instead of hoarded if women look on time as something precious, and help each other to use it more effectively.

No one advocates living less graciously; no one wants husbands and children to be neglected or deprived. Yet in the pace of today's world it is evident that all citizens have ever wider responsibilities. As women see that they have much to contribute to their community, mothers may want to take a new look at their household tasks. How could these be done more simply? Are all of them really necessary? Would a little rearrangement here and there give considerably more time? What tasks can be shared with neighbors to the easement of all? Could one person do the ironing, for example, both for herself and the next-door neighbor? Next week she would have a morning free while her neighbor ironed.

"If we could only realize that we don't need to provide dozens of different sorts of dishes at every meal," admitted an Egyptian.

"Just grinding our spices may take three hours," commented a Malaysian.

Once women were content to fill their days with spice-grinding and a steady round of kitchen chores. Now many are not quite so sure.

"Once our position was simple . . . now we begin to see that there is more."

❀

Six

The World of Working Women

No longer is "Should women work?" a question for consideration. They are doing it by the millions, either for pay or as volunteers. The questions now are:

How can women serve their families best?
How can they best develop and fulfill themselves?
How can they contribute most to society?

Every society draws relatively firm lines as to what is man's work and what is woman's. However, there is a wide difference of opinion as to which job belongs in whose lap. In some cultures women weave but men do not; other people reverse this. Women are the traders in some areas, whereas elsewhere they may not even do the marketing for the household. In some countries women carry bricks and mortar and heavy building materials up ladders on construction jobs. In the U.S.S.R. women are also sailors. In other lands these are considered types of work only for men.

But as machines tend to reduce the physical strength required in many jobs, young girls can handle what once was impossible for them. Fields of work are also opening up through new scientific developments which have not yet been assigned a sex, so are open to all. Wars have forced both men and women to take each other's jobs. The world has seen women fighting fires, serving as railway porters, handling heavy mails, packing parachutes, running trains. A woman in Karachi, Pakistan, owns and operates a cement factory; another in Burma has been director of one of the country's largest rice concerns; one in New York directs a shipping company. There appears to be no biological reason and no fixed social reason why women cannot make their contribution to society on any level, in almost any occupation.

For better or worse, the trend of social change appears to be towards women working outside their homes for at least some part of their lives. Much of this trend is due to increasing costs of living as demands for more education and higher standards of living spread. Sometimes loneliness and boredom rather than the need for money lure women to the satisfaction and companionship of jobs. Other women—as for example many nurses—work from a sense of obligation to society. But by and large, the great majority of women who work do so because they need the money. Their greatest job satisfaction lies in the cash it brings, the goods it buys, the sense of independence it gives.

In the United States, contrary to most people's idea of American women, about thirty-five million of the married women devote their full time to homemaking. Almost one-third of all married women, and many single women as well, are both workers and homemakers.[1] The important thing to realize is that women's work outside their homes is no longer merely a matter of conflicting family responsibilities or of what they want to do for their own personal finances. The fact now is that women are needed in the fast-growing economies of most countries.

Dr. Helga Pross, a sociologist of West Germany, has made this observation:

> Nowhere in the industrialized territories, neither in Europe nor in the United States, or in the Soviet Union, the national economy could function efficiently without women cooperating as workers, clerks, civil servants, farmers, educators, and so forth. In West Germany, we now have a female labor force of approximately seven million. To withdraw these seven millions from their jobs would lead to an almost complete breakdown of factories, offices, and schools.[2]

Dr. Mohei-el-Din Saber, writing of woman, says: "She is in fact a non-existing entity in the social and economic life of certain Arab countries. This leaves society to breathe with one lung and work with one arm, thus . . . reflecting negatively on the industrial income rate and leaving the man as sole provider of the family needs."[3]

In rural areas women have always shared the work in the fields. An International Labor Organization report indicates that in India in 1958 12.5 million women were supporting themselves as hired labor, working either full or part time; twenty million more were "earning dependents" on their own land; and over thirty-nine million were non-earning dependents.[4]

A special problem occurs in many countries where industrialization is growing, because rural wives are separated from their husbands when the men migrate to the cities. Women tend to stay behind to maintain the farms. Therefore, they are often the stabilizing factor in rural economics that helps to feed the population and make industrialization possible during a transitional period; although the separation often causes major social hardships.

Many countries are creating aids to help women enter the

business and labor worlds where their skills and contributions are needed.

Although a Moslem country, Indonesia has not had most of the restrictive customs which affect the social life of most Moslem nations. As a result, the world's third most populated country offers women a broad range of activities.

In the city of Djakarta alone there are thirteen women's banks, including one operated by the women's organization, Kongress Wanita. These banks are operated specifically to help women with their savings and investments; they give counseling services to women planning to start businesses; they help to arrange emergency loans for business enterprises if these are being carried out by women.

Other countries, too, work to improve women's financial sense and assist them in setting out on their own economic ventures. Many banks in the United States have counselors whose job it is to help women handle their finances wisely. Switzerland operates substantial loan funds specifically for women to help them start their own businesses. In West Africa, societies like the Port Loko Thrift Society, in Freetown, Sierra Leone, have been doing the same since 1959. Members have borrowed to build houses or to buy sewing machines. They have taken out loans to pay for their children's schooling, buy business equipment, or extend their marketing areas.

The value of such arrangements can be assessed in terms of more than economic contribution. There is also substantial value in the realm of increased self-reliance and independence.

In many parts of the world Women's Co-operative Societies are helping to ease the transition for women between the responsibilities of their homes and those of the business world. Some "co-ops" help women to save on transportation, or to develop markets; they guarantee profitable sales in pig-raising, poultry-farming, sisal-growing, and the like. Others help develop handcrafts or provide outlets for selling foods which women can preserve at home.

Egypt contributes this account:

> We now have a Co-operative Society for working mothers who cannot leave home. They can make goods at home, then sell them through the Co-operative which:
> 1. Makes a loan to start the home industry (thereby eliminating the "middle man" with his high interest rates).
> 2. Provides raw materials at wholesale prices.
> 3. Helps to market the final product at the best possible prices.
>
> Meanwhile, [the report continues] members receive interest on their shares and are encouraged to work at home where they can keep an eye on their children.[5]

It should, however, be recognized that the market for handcrafts is diminishing. As factories improve their standards and drastically reduce prices, handmade goods, although beautiful, find it increasingly difficult to compete in the world's markets. Perhaps young women would do well to consider shifting their emphasis to the areas of service rather than crafts. More of them might better use their time to prepare for skills such as hairdressing, dressmaking, catering, bookkeeping, and selling rather than embroidery or the traditional skills.

In some areas small local factories are providing another partial answer to women's needs for added income during the time when their children are small. A number of them distribute piecework which can be done at home. This can be a helpful source of income to mothers, but women should be alert to the dangers of exploitation in this kind of work. If they are not getting adequate pay for the work done, they should gather in a united front to make their requirements firm.

Although the debate continues as to whether or not it is bad for families if the mother works, there is in actual fact no rule of right or wrong. It varies. How young are the children? Is she a widow or divorcée supporting a family? Has she skills, ability, and creativity to give to society? Does she live on a farm or in a town? What does her husband think, and what is he able to provide for the family? Is she offending her culture by her work?

Mrs. Rita de Bruyn Ouboter, Chairman of the International Council of Social Democratic Women, believes young mothers often are right to be working outside the home.

> I grant that many mothers who hold a job and also have young children have many difficulties to overcome, but it is equally important to stress the advantages to be gained by participation in the country's economic life. This may give women a broader outlook, especially if they have had a better education. Furthermore, there can be advantages also for the children, to whom their mothers may be able to give a better education. This may be more important in the long run than the fact that the children may suffer now and then a feeling of loneliness or of being neglected.[6]

In the United States one-third of the nation's working people are women; the majority of them are married (or have been). There are often serious psychological factors caused by raising a family while at the same time working to supplement a husband's income. This is often an inescapable necessity, however, especially for those in lower income groups.

Dr. Pross says:

> One possible solution I believe to be . . . education. To teach young girls how to read and write, and how to become efficient secretaries, workers, physicians, teachers or what else is not enough. Some additional psychological instruction is

> needed. . . . Women must learn to decide by themselves. Also, they must be made conscious of the fact that one cannot have everything at every time, that is, have all the gratifications of married life and the advantages of a career life as well. . . . Finally, girls and adult women must be given better instruction on how to organize their life and particularly on how to plan the housework. No doubt that married women need not spend all day at home, but could have plenty of spare hours for other activities, if they were more efficient in organizing their work.[7]

One of the significant developments in the United States in women's education is the greatly increased number of adult women who are going back to school and college after their children are grown and their family responsibilities have become lighter. The same is happening in Egypt, Great Britain, and elsewhere. Because such women provide a new and badly needed source of trained power for the nation, a growing number of colleges are setting up special programs to help women qualify for useful jobs in the nation's labor force. If they qualify, women of any age are welcome to begin or to complete college courses; alumnae are offered special privileges to attend "adult" courses; vocational workshops are set up to help older college graduates who now want to work outside their homes.

Says Mrs. Millicent C. McIntosh, former President of Barnard College, who pioneered much of this new development in the United States:

> The period of women's rights has merged into the period of women's opportunities. . . . A truly cultivated mind is not incompatible with femininity or with the married estate.[8]

There are many specific ways in which countries can give support to women who must do outside work, but who also strive to keep a happy home.

PERSONNEL PRACTICES

Nations will never tap the full reserves of feminine energy and talent until employers become more flexible in their personnel practices in order to allow for the double role that most women play. Elina Huttunen of Finland offered this specific recommendation:

> More women might work on a team basis—each working a half day to cover the job, but each able in this way to handle her own home responsibilities better. Many jobs lend themselves easily to being divided. The workers could be paired, each doing a half day's work in such occupations as: switchboard operators, elevator girls, waitresses, factory jobs, sales clerks, copy-typists, beauticians.
>
> When people understand that there is profit for the firm in such a system, much will be won. A half day's work without the lunch hour is cheaper for the employer. It is true, the employee will not get as much money in salary, of course, but she will be well compensated by time won for her home and family. Furthermore, when she has time to do her own housework and to shop carefully, her money will stretch further.[9]

DAY NURSERIES

"What we need more than anything else are adequate and inexpensive places for small children at or near the place of work, or attached to housing areas," said women of Korea at a conference held there.[10]

"For the older children, free school meals would make a great difference," said a Swedish group.

EMERGENCY HOME WORKERS

As noted elsewhere, the Scandinavians, aware of the worry and female absenteeism caused by children's illness at home, have developed the Emergency Home Helpers. This Corps is available on call to run a home if there is a need.

"It is cheaper for us to maintain a staff of nurses to go out to our workers' homes," said the Director of Arabia, a pottery factory in Finland, "than it is to have the losses of absent workers. Meanwhile the mother maintains her income while we continue to benefit from her skill."

HOME SERVICES

Part of the reason why the women of the United States appear to be so emancipated is that mass-produced clothing, modern food-processing, the supermarket, and all the wonders of drip-dry textiles have meant a tremendous saving in their domestic time and energy. Clean, attractive homes and good meals for their families do not require more than a fraction of the time they once did. Such household aids are fast appearing in other parts of the world and will continue to do so. More and more women are discovering that, thanks to new devices, they have increasing amounts of free time which they can now devote to the community or the working world without lowering their standards at home. They realize the fresh new opportunities this provides.

NEW DIRECTIONS

There are other factors which can make a great difference to women's contribution to their nation's growing economies:

TRADE UNIONS

Too few women, as yet, are playing a major role in trade unions, yet these exist to improve conditions for their members. In some countries women are contributing greatly, but many others are still unaware of protective labor laws that already do exist.

VALUE ON HOUSEWORK

The economic value of household duties is not sufficiently recognized by either men or women themselves. Perhaps retirement benefits and similar benefits will be developed for housewives as their worth to nations is made apparent. The Italian Parliament has already approved a scheme establishing a plan for old-age pensions for housewives.

TO MEET AUTOMATION

Technical training is urgently needed for women as well as for men if, as seems likely, machines are going to change the whole pattern of unskilled and semiskilled work all over the world.

LONG-TERM, LOW-INTEREST LOANS

Loans of this type, easily available, were stressed as a major need by Latin-American women taking part in the Bogotá United Nations Seminar so that people could buy more labor-saving machinery.

The same point was later raised by the women of Africa, when they met at Addis Ababa in 1960. They made a formal plea for governments or co-operatives to provide:

> Small, electric-powered mills to relieve them of the slow, exhausting, repetitive task of milling grain daily with heavy pestle and mortar.
>
> Pipes, bore-holes, and wells, so that women could be relieved of the drudgery of carrying water for long weary miles on their backs and heads.

Seven

What Is Ahead for Working Women?

THERE IS NO question that women have a steadily increasing impact on society through their work. Mr. John Charles Roche, Lecturer in Business Administration at the Royal College in Nairobi, Kenya, points it up this way:

> In advancing countries there are women who reach top-level positions, but it is those at the intermediate level who have made the greatest impact. (Women run large firms in Europe and America, but the thousands of women . . . secretaries have had a major effect on business efficiency.)
>
> We have women doctors who raised the prestige of women, but it is the nurses who humanized hospital treatment.
>
> Famous women professors have contributed [to] scholarship, but the body of women teachers in elementary schools had the greater effect on national progress.[1]

From culture to culture and nation to nation, there is, of course, considerable variation in the ways in which women are making their greatest economic contributions. Generally speaking, however, women's work falls into the following categories:

EDUCATION

This is the traditional profession into which women first go. It continues to absorb by far the greatest numbers in both old and new countries alike. Here, through the teaching profession, women can exert their greatest influence on social and economic change; here they have the greatest opportunity to make a lasting contribution through the training of a future generation.

MEDICINE

Following teaching comes professional nursing and the allied fields of midwifery and medical technology. Much more help is needed in this field.

At the first of the United Nations Seminars on the "Participation of Women in Public Life" held in Bangkok in 1957, Asian women discussed this matter at some length. One of their formally adopted conclusions was:

> The acute shortage of doctors, nurses, nurses' aides, medical social workers and trained midwives, as well as the training and supervision of traditional birth attendants requires the urgent attention of governments, voluntary organizations and individual citizens. Besides adequate professional training, attention should be focused on the development of the sense of civic responsibility, dedication to service and emotional preparation for the type of locality and people with whom health and welfare workers are going to work.
>
> Consideration should also be given to the housing, conditions of work, salaries, and status in the community of all health and welfare workers.[2]

FARM WORK

Roughly 80 per cent of the world's people live in rural communities. Women have always been an economic asset on farms. One sees them working in the wheatfields of Yugoslavia, the rubber plantations of Liberia, the coffee hills of Brazil, the rice paddies of Japan, and the hopfields of England. All over the world, from earliest times, women have sowed and tilled and harvested along with their men—poorly paid, exhausted, but working hard.

Today a threat hangs over them. New methods of tilling the soil, tending the crops, reaping the harvest, are raising each acre's yield and providing more food. Machines are cutting down the backbreaking, endless hard day's labor. Within twenty years, less than half of those presently working on farms will be required.

This is a challenge not only for governments but also for local communities. Those who think and plan ahead will establish vocational training now for the children who would have been tomorrow's farm workers. Women's organizations may well consider, "what will our own women do a few years from now when farm machines are more available?" Some of the answers may lie in the field of commercial canning and preserving. More women may go into industries such as pressing oils and making wines, manufacturing raw sugar, or the culture of silk—industries allied to their experience. But if such shifts of labor are to occur smoothly, training, planning, and preparation should soon get under way.

WORK IN RURAL AREAS

And what of those who work in services in rural areas? Miss Ruth Woodsmall has this to say:

> Securing women personnel for health service in rural communities presents the familiar problem of the shortage of women candidates willing to enter service in rural areas, in view of prevailing social conservatism. All candidates, in varying degrees, face the same difficulties in living conditions and a generally adverse social climate, especially for unmarried women. . . . A change in social conditions is a necessity.[3]

Material comforts are not the only question. Boredom is another big factor which keeps energetic, alert young people from going into rural work. The dean of a Middle Eastern women's college says:

> Our girls would like to work in the way that would best help the country—this would be in the village. But what will they do there in their free time? How will they spend their time when they are not actually working? We must solve this problem before we can recruit educated girls or men to work well in the rural areas.[4]

THE REST OF THE PICTURE

Other broad areas in which women's skills are predominant, or a major factor, are: clerical, services, industry, sales.

Trading, of course, is an area in which tens of thousands of women support themselves in many areas, such as West Africa. There the market is largely a women's world.

Writes Daniel F. McCall:

> The market is largely a woman's world; it is her club as well as her means of livelihood. She spends most of the day sitting by a table or a basket of goods, gossiping, plaiting a friend's hair, or having her own done, and incidentally making sales. A woman would rather be a trader than a farmer if she has the choice; it is an easier and more social life.
>
> The number of women engaged in trading has been constantly growing. In the old days, most of the men were farmers and their wives also worked on the farm; together they raised almost everything that was necessary for their subsistence. Today a man gives his wife or wives a sum of money as part of the marriage settlement and she is expected to provide for herself on the proceeds of the trading that she can carry on with that amount.[5]

In all of these broad categories there is much room for planning. New developments provide new opportunities.

Technology is having a tremendous effect. During the next few decades it is certain that the changes will come at an ever-faster rate, beyond anything we can now predict.

WAGES

Changes are occurring, too, in salaries and benefits. In general, women do not receive as much income from their work as men. This results partly from tradition, partly because it is assumed that their first allegiance is to their home, rather than to their job; men do not expect them to be as dedicated in their careers. Often, girls' education has lagged behind that of men so that they have been limited to low-wage occupations.

However, all this is gradually changing. Equal-pay clauses are increasingly being included in collective bargaining agreements; national labor policies are acknowledging women's rights; the International Labor Organization has been working to eliminate wage practices that discriminate against women. The first countries to ratify an equal-pay convention were: Austria, Belgium, Dominican Republic, France, Mexico, and Yugoslavia. France established minimum wage rates for men and women in 1945, and accepted the "equal pay for equal work" principle in the following year.

Thirty-eight nations, including U.S.S.R., have signed the International Labor Organization charter on equal pay for equal work. Women of Singapore were granted equal pay in 1962. Britain has accepted the principle for government workers, teachers, and other professional people, and steady pressure is being continued in other areas of work by the determined women of the United Kingdom. As yet, only sixteen of the fifty states of the United States have laws requiring equal pay for women, whereas it has been taken for granted in Burma since the days of ancient kings that women would be given equal return for equal work. The delicate-looking Burmese women, with lovely flowers tucked into their glossy black hair, have always been actively engaged in all walks of life. They have long held positions of responsibility in business, industry, professions, the diplomatic service, and throughout Burma's whole structure.

Employers frequently object that women are costlier as workers in the long run. Marriage often terminates a woman's usefulness, so her training and experience go with her. If she does stay on, the employer may have to pay her during several months of maternity leave which, as far as the office is concerned, is unproductive. Women's demand for equal pay is sometimes held against them in seeking jobs. Sometimes, an appointment which might have been given to a woman goes to a man instead.

"Exploitation" is the cry on the other side. "Some employers have dismissed male workers and taken on women staff because they can pay them less to do the same work," accuses the National Union of Plantation Workers.

Recently, in the Malaysian press, a spokesman for the Ministry of Labor said: "Women are proving to be such good workers in several industries in Malaya that the bosses now tend to employ them in preference to men. . . . Even in some jobs where they are paid less than men, they earn more than men by working harder."[6]

SOCIAL SECURITY

The concept of social security—public programs of health insurance and other forms of assistance—is about eighty years old. The first compulsory social insurance act was passed in Germany in 1883. The last twenty years have seen social security programs spreading rapidly to all parts of the world, reaching many millions of people. The five usual types of protection are:

1. Old age, survivors', and disability insurance.
2. Health and maternity care.
3. Workmen's compensation (for injuries received on the job).
4. Unemployment insurance.
5. Family allowances.

Of particular interest to women are national health and maternity programs. Thousands of women have contributed endless volunteer hours to bringing such programs repeatedly before legislatures, and mobilizing public opinion to support the need for such protection. By 1955, forty-five countries had set up such programs. Included among them were Italy, Spain, Turkey, Formosa, Australia, India, Nicaragua, and Peru.

In Great Britain, the National Health Service (which has been carefully studied and adapted by many other countries) brought in sweeping universal health provisions for everyone. Medical care has been extended in recent years not only to workers but also to their whole families in Bulgaria, Chile, Ecuador, Ireland, Japan, and Luxembourg.

Another form of government financial assistance particularly affecting wives and mothers lies in the realm of family allowance programs. These have been spreading across the world, adding to the cash income of families with children. New Zealand, Belgium, and France were the first to start such programs. In most of the British Commonwealth and the Scandinavian countries, allowances are paid to all families with a specified number of children. Denmark and South

Africa give allowances only to low-income families. In most other countries, family allowances are more like a supplement to wages, relating to one's employer, not to one's government.

There is some concern that such allowances may be doing harm in that they encourage people to have large families. Others say that the amounts given are not large enough to encourage increased families but that they do help to support children and minimize hardship once they are born.

An interesting suggestion was made at the 1959 Bogotá United Nations Seminar that family allowances should be granted only when children are actually sent to school, thus stimulating parents to send their children to be educated, rather than using their labor at home. The Mayor of Rio de Janeiro is already trying the experiment and believes it to be effective.

By no means everything that has been developed in the older, industrialized countries is necessarily appropriate in other countries. Greater security may be given to more people, for example, if a country concentrates on creating conditions of full employment, rather than spending large sums on unemployment insurance. During the early stages of national growth, such an insurance plan may be an economic luxury that a country cannot afford.

The concept of making people stop work at a certain age and then giving them a pension for life also needs to be considered carefully. This system was established in the United States and elsewhere when jobs were scarce; older people were replaced to make room at the top for others to move upwards. But in a period of full employment, it can be wasteful of good talent. A better pattern for some countries might be to enable older people to move gradually into situations where they can work at lessened pace, rather than under full pressure. In this way their education and experience can still be useful, even while their energies taper off.

THE NEXT INDUSTRIAL REVOLUTION

Countries which are just starting to develop their industries have the advantage of being able to learn from the mistakes of countries which have been working at it longer. In this way they can protect their people from the beginning against many of the major hazards of an industrial economy.

One of these hazards is child labor. This evil is still widespread in many nations. Small children can be found at work in cold, dark buildings, crouched on plank scaffoldings as they work on beautiful handmade rugs or embroidery. Others stand for long hours wrapping candies, sorting coffee beans, or doing other routine chores. While economic levels remain as perilously close to starvation as many of them do, the few coins these children earn are a necessity for family survival, but they are earned at a terrible cost to the next generation.

The International Labor Organization has done great work in establishing modern labor standards. The law is one thing, however; observance of it is something else. Here is where public opinion can be important. The public can help to eliminate unnecessary evils: eyes and ears and the pressure of public opinion can do much to see that the law is obeyed.

Other areas also need watchful attention on the part of the public—especially women—as more and more of them move into factories. Some of these are:

The length of working weeks and working days.
Wage minimums.
Health and safety standards in factories, including rest

periods, places where workers can sit and rest, and adequate sanitary facilities.

Opportunities for part-time work for mothers of households.

Adequate hostels for single working women.

Day-care facilities for the children of working mothers.

If working women do not group together to make demands; if educated women do not help them with the support of their education and abilities (for example helping to bring about needed legislation) the women of the newly industrializing countries will go through the same hardships that befell their sisters in earlier periods in other lands. There is no need for the same mistakes to be made now. What is required is vigilance.

Throughout most of history, the human economy has been one of scarcity. Every waking hour had to be used for survival—building, plowing, weaving, collecting fuel, carrying water. Until the time of the Industrial Revolution, there were but few people in the world for whom life was more than a hard, endless round of work. People had to make their own candles and shoes; spin their own thread; raise their own crops; make their own lumber or bricks; shape their own implements; repair their own tools. In those days, women's labor was needed in the home just to get through the daily necessities. This is still true in great areas of today's world. Many a woman's day still begins at dawn and carries on in both field and home until darkness sends her to bed.

But as scarcity is eliminated and replaced by plenty, as machines replace repetitive tasks about the home and ease the labor of the fields, women can rise. More and more of them are steadily being freed from grinding through the same heavy round day after day, year after year, from birth to premature old age.

Meanwhile, stemming originally from the American and French Revolutions, the stirring ideas of human dignity, human equality, and human rights—including education for women as well as men—have been leading the world into new directions. Democracy, socialism, even communism, all promise human emancipation. Whether the promise is kept or not, the idea grows in people's minds.

"Emancipation" in practice (not merely theory) includes the possibilities of work at a job of one's choice in a place of one's choice; the material benefits of earning; the freedom attained by the possession of some income, however small. Through the decades women are becoming more free. They are moving out beside men increasingly into nearly all fields of human endeavor:

To earn money, thereby helping to ease or improve their family's standards of living.

To contribute to their country's shifting economy.

To take part in the stir and ferment which always occurs when people taste the heady wine of freedom, respect, and equal treatment.

❀

Eight

What One Person Can Do

DR. JOHN W. GARDNER, a well-known American educator, writes:

> It is my conviction that free and responsible individuals are proud to offer such devotion if given the opportunity. People would rather work hard for something they believe in than enjoy a pampered idleness. . . . Every free man, in his work and in his family life, in his public behavior and in the secret places of his heart, should see himself as a builder and maintainer of the ideals of his society. . . . How does one contribute to the greatness and strength of a free society? That is a question to which there are many true answers. One answer is—pursue excellence! . . . The man who does his job well tones up the whole society. And the man who does a slovenly job—whether he is a janitor or a judge, a surgeon or a technician—lowers the tone of the society. So do the chiselers of high and low degree, the sleight-of-hand artists who know how to gain an advantage without honest work. They are the regrettable burdens of a free society.[1]

Despite all the complexities of modern life, the most important factor still remains the individual human spirit.

The astronomer was asked: "When you think in terms of the immensity of space, the distances measured by light years, when you contemplate the planets and the stars, the age of the celestial bodies, what is Man?" The astronomer's reply was quiet and simple. "Man," he said, "is the astronomer."

In talking about majestic, world-sweeping ideals, most people tend to talk in terms of men. But let us look at some of the ways in which women also are trying to bridge all kinds of dividing barriers—those of tribe or race; those of national heritage or language; of caste or class; of religion or color; the divisions between educated and uneducated; city or village; rich or poor. Women are concerned with the great human questions of our time. Some of those concerned are so-called "important" people; many are quite unknown; some are schooled, some are not; some are in cities and work in organized groups; others are individuals working alone. The one quality that they all have in common is that they care; therefore they work. They are "toning up" society by what they are doing. Let us meet a few of them and see examples of the many ways in which individuals are quietly working.

SHE WORKS WITH HER PEN

Elsa Arana is a journalist in Peru. Like so many other cities throughout the world, Lima, Peru's capital, has a fast-growing slum area, spreading out on all sides of the city. As desperately poor Indians and mountain people crowd in, seeking jobs and a new life, more and more miserable tar-paper and scrap-tin shanties are built to give them shelter. Here they live, crowded, dirty, half-starved, rat-ridden. Water is hard to get; there is no light; illness is everywhere.

Elsa Arana heard officials talk about these conditions, but she saw no action being taken to improve them. "I will take it to the people," she said to herself. "If the people can be sufficiently aroused it will force official action." The men of her newspaper agreed; they said they would carry her story even though it might be politically unpopular.

Elsa did not start to write until she really knew her subject. She moved in with the people. She lived for weeks in her own tumble-down shanty atop the city garbage heap. Rats ran over her as she slept; she stood long hours in line with her neighbors as they waited for water at the single faucet. She talked and listened; she helped the people around her as they went through the crises of life—childbirth and death. She "felt with her skin." Then she began to write. She told not only of conditions, but of what these do to human souls. She had living stories to tell. The paper printed it—all of it. Every day for seven days in succession, they carried a full-page spread, with pictures, telling all that Elsa had seen and learned and felt. The impact was powerful. Other papers picked up the story and carried it; wire services were interested. Israel and Spain wrote, inviting her to receive their awards for outstanding journalism. Elsa went off to accept these honors. Meanwhile the stories were reprinted and reread; they began to spread. The result: city officials have begun to put in electricity and better water supplies. But the story is not finished. Elsa, working with her editors, will see that it is not.

SHE WORKS FAR FROM HOME

In Ballah, twenty miles from Ilorin, in Nigeria, the village chief, dressed in striking robes, leads his entourage to greet pink-cheeked Miss Crowley of Ireland. A local official solemnly rings a great bell, whereupon fifty or sixty women, surrounded by wide-eyed babies and children, gather in the square. A table is put in the shade of a baobab tree and soon the whole group are engrossed in learning the simple principles of hygiene; chatter increases as they busy themselves in cooking nutritious meals with the local foods they have carried in themselves. Washing plates, bathing babies, sweeping compounds, keeping goats and chickens out of the huts, covering children from flies, and raising cooking utensils off

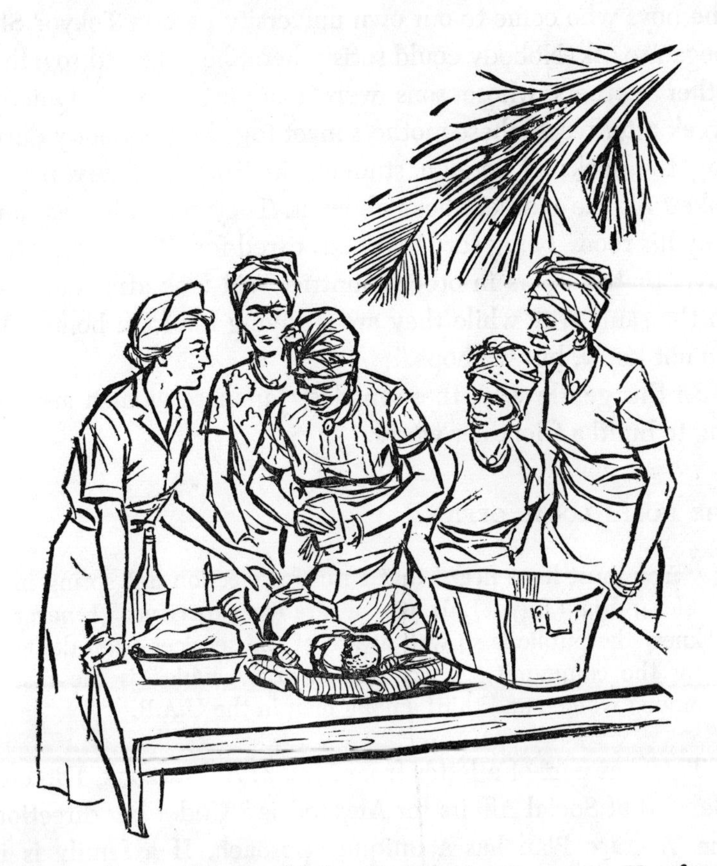

the ground are all part of Miss Crowley's campaign. Far from her Irish home she, and hundreds like her, steadily do the world's work for F.A.O., U.N.I.C.E.F., church groups, or other agencies which are trying to help people raise the level of their own lives all over the world.[2]

QUIETLY THEY CARE

A kimono-clad mother in Tokyo worried about her son who had gone to study in San Francisco. Who would look after him? How could he get along without his mother—or a wife—to tend to his needs? Suddenly she thought: who looks after the boys who come to our own university here in Tokyo? She began to ask. Nobody could satisfy her. She gathered together other mothers whose sons were studying abroad. Quietly, week after week, these mothers meet together, patiently darning the socks of foreign students in Tokyo. If any boy is taken ill, the mothers hear about it. They take him tea, and tidy his room, being sure that he is cared for. "We hope," they say, "that mothers in other countries will look after our sons in the same way while they are studying far from home. We do not know, but we hope."

In this gentle way, these modest Japanese women are trying to build a friendlier world.

SHE HOLDS LOCAL OFFICE

> You must have heard that I ran for election last spring in Alexandria (Egypt). It was a strange experience. I never knew the public is so well aware of the services I am doing for the community. I won 24,000 votes, which is the first among women and third among men in the U.A.R.

This was part of a letter from Mrs. Z. A. Marzouk, Director General of Social Affairs for Alexandria.[3] Under her direction, the Welfare Plan has a unique approach. If a family is in need and accepted by the Welfare Department, the entire family is assisted to the utmost. As many members of the family as possible will be given vocational training; all will be given every kind of medical care—teeth, eyes, everything.

But at the end of one year they are supposed to be on their feet, able to fend for themselves from that time on. Mrs. Marzouk explains:

> We help them get started, but they know they have a limited time. This gives them great incentive and seems to work well. We do not approve of carrying the same people on our welfare roles for years if they will not work to help themselves. But first they must be helped to believe in themselves. Nothing will happen without that belief, and without reasonably good health.[4]

For many years this energetic woman has campaigned with authorities and with the public to extend welfare to the people of her city in the way that will benefit them most in spirit as well as in body.

SHE HOLDS NATIONAL OFFICE

A woman Member of Parliament in Sweden writes:

> I am exhausted after the adoption of our new criminal act. I was a member of the Standing Committee that had many objections to some of the principal questions regarding the treatment of the young criminal in our country. We had been working with people concerned with youth, delinquency, with prisons, with schools for vocational training and the like.
>
> I had to take the floor directly after our Minister of Justice, and I suppose you can imagine how that must have felt. It was like waiting for an execution, I sometimes felt, seeing day after day pass, and knowing there remained only five, four, three, two days to H hour. Nevertheless, I am told I did a good job of it. Some of my objections were taken by chambers, so the amendments from me are to be put into the legal texts instead of the original. I did not succeed fully in all respects. I am aghast at the thought that we can put a boy of fifteen in prison, meeting grownups with grave criminal records. At least my criticisms of this made them consider and

> write exactly when and why you do this in exceptional cases, and stress the point of restriction, so my defeat was itself not wholly unsuccessful. But afterward I fell together like a balloon that you have pricked with a needle![5]

This woman made her contribution by her refusal to compromise with principles she felt were right. She was willing to fight for them though it felt "like waiting for an execution."

THE SCHOOLED AND THE UNSCHOOLED

Sometimes one person who cares "sparks" those around her, and thus gets much accomplished that she could not do alone. Such a one was the teen-age head of the Student Council in a New Jersey high school in the United States. This girl was restless for the time when she would be old enough to get out into the world and be useful. Then she realized that there were already ways in which she could mobilize her own friends and get something done. She did not have to wait. She had read about the U.N.E.S.C.O. Gift Coupon Plan for use in the developing countries.

There is a joint council for three hundred high schools in New Jersey so that they can work together on any matter which concerns them all. This world-minded girl persuaded the key members of this council that they should undertake an overseas project. U.N.E.S.C.O. assigned them "Project 344," which happens to be a primary school for young girls in Garango, Upper Volta, in the heart of the semidesert area of West Africa. A 150-mile road links Garango with Upper Volta's capital, Ouagedougou; however, communications are so bad that it is often two weeks between mail deliveries. Only a small percentage of Upper Volta's children go to school; of those few, only about a third are girls. The few girls in a mixed school were confused and miserable under the pressures of a society which traditionally saw no place for educated women. It was reported that nothing they learned seemed to have any relationship with the everyday life of the community, and they were rapidly overwhelmed by the lethargy around them. They resigned themselves to their fate, but not without the vague feeling of being somehow cheated. After a few years, no one could guess that they had ever been to school. Who would see that the girls had a role to play in Upper Volta? Who would help them to discover their own capabilities? A school of their own, with a curriculum designed especially for their own needs, was clearly required.

In 1959, an International Team was sent out consisting of a French nurse and two Canadian teachers. That first class held seventy girls, ranging in age from eight to ten years old. Now this group has moved on to a secondary school in the capital; the hope is that many of them will return to Garango and its neighboring villages to teach others.

Once they had selected Project 344, the New Jersey students became engrossed in that Upper Volta school. They read and learned and studied about all of West Africa; to raise money for "their" school in Garango they held dances; the girls baked and sold cakes; they put on book fairs; they held all sorts of contests and competitions and rallies. Slowly the bank account grew until, through U.N.E.S.C.O., they were able to turn over more than $4,000 to help towards the building of a center, to buy teaching materials, to provide sports equipment, and also the essentials for a badly needed clinic. The school is growing and making an impact in the area.

"In one great leap," writes the Canadian Directress of the school, "these girls have passed from a gloomy and passive traditional timidity to a marvellous spontaneity. . . . They show a joyful eagerness to participate."[6]

THE POWER OF A BOYCOTT

Housewives all over the world grumble over the way the cost of living continually skyrockets far beyond incomes. Generally grumbling is all they do, but occasionally, because of one concerned individual, more effective action is taken. One determined woman can change the whole trend. This has been proved in Tokyo, Dublin, Singapore, Oslo, and elsewhere.

In these cities, when prices have risen too high and too fast, a single housewife has more than once goaded others into joint action to tackle the problem. Gathering the strength of numbers as they proceed, they have divided the city into zones, canvassed the merchants, and arranged for concessions for all housewives holding special identity cards. Discounts as high as ten per cent on textiles, foods, medicines, and toys have sometimes been forthcoming from shopkeepers who wanted to keep the women's trade. As memberships grew, a boycott of those shops which were not willing to cut prices always became more and more powerful. Shopkeepers can hardly ever afford to ignore a great mass of determined women. The upward spiral of costs has, in several instances, been visibly slowed.

A specific example lies in the Consumers Resistance Movement in Singapore, which drew public attention to spiraling costs immediately after the war.

The first definite step taken was the establishment of a Co-operative Store which undersold its competitors. Quickly the Consumers Resistance Movement exposed profiteers and black marketeers to public view and forced the removal of "middle men" who had been reaping handsome profits while leaving little revenue for the hard-working men and women who actually produced the goods.

Work of this watchful sort on the part of citizens is part of the price of national freedom.

How else can "watchdog" systems work?

"Shopping Panels" are sometimes developed to cover every area of a city. Teams of women are assigned to go through the stores at regular intervals, checking on quality and prices, keeping their members informed of any "discoveries," good or bad, through a monthly newsletter:

"In this shop the weights are inaccurate."

"This shop is well-lit; the proprietor is courteous and has a good quality of merchandise."

"Here the merchandise is dirty."

"There the prices are too high."

Those who read do their shopping accordingly. The power of thousands of women buying or not buying from their shops has a healthy influence on merchants. They tend to conform to higher standards of quality and cleanliness and also to lower their prices under the bright light of public exposure.

This type of pressure for the public good is not too difficult to organize. It takes *someone who cares* to start the ball rolling; it takes a spirit of teamwork; but it can be done effectively with no equipment and no funds—only energy and determination.

ONE IDEA CHANGED A TOWN

In a town in East Pakistan where transportation was an acute problem, gentle, sari-clad women gathered together at a social tea given by one of the organizations.

"My husband will not allow me to use public transport," said one. "So I can never volunteer in anything."

"My husband lets me use his car," said another, "but I never

know when I can have it, so I can never be regular in attendance."

"It takes me an hour to get to the kindergarten where I like to work," said another, "and an hour to get home, so I hardly ever go."

The picture unfolded of half-hearted spasmodic use of their free time for community activities, although all the ladies speaking were leisured, wealthy, educated—and restless. They could have helped enormously with many needs of their struggling city.

One of the women listened quietly to the various reasons and excuses that were being offered. Everything seemed to center around the problem of getting regularly to the places where these women might usefully contribute their hours and their energy.

At the next meeting she produced a map of the town, together with a box of pins with colored heads. She spread it out on a table and asked, "Where are the various kindergartens, clinics, prisons, food distribution centers, hospitals, remand homes, orphanages, etc., located?" Together they stuck pins in the map, covering every welfare activity known to anyone present. When they had finished, pins were scattered widely over the map.

She took out a box of pins with different colored heads.

"Now where does each one of you live?" she asked. Again heads bent low over the map, as each person present located her home and stuck in a pin to indicate. Gradually her plan became visible before them.

"Oh," said one, "I could work at that clinic on the next block, couldn't I?"

"I never knew there was a kindergarten in that house on my corner," said another.

"There is a food depot near me," agreed another, "but it is not run by my organization so I could not volunteer there."

"Why not?" she was asked.

"Well, I don't know. I could try. Do you suppose they would use me?"

At the end of the meeting, the bored and restless ladies went home with a new enthusiasm. Instead of feeling trapped by the unsurmountable problem of getting themselves transported around town, they suddenly realized that they could be useful after all; that there was a place for them in their own locality, that without any drastic change, they could fill their lives with new interest and so become a part of their city's life and growth.

One woman with one idea . . .

Dag Hammarskjöld, late Secretary General of the United Nations, recognized well the vital importance of the individual. In his New Year's message, December 31, 1953, he put the task squarely:

> Our work for peace must begin within the private world of each one of us. To build for man a world without fear, *we* must be without fear. To build a world of justice, *we* must be just. And how can we fight for liberty if we are not free in our own minds? How can we ask others to sacrifice if *we* are not ready to do so?[7]

John Gardner itemizes the immediate tasks near at hand for each one of us. Everyone of us can make some contribution regarding at least one of these problems once we realize that many solutions lie within us, the individual people of the world. He writes that there are:

> Still too many children trapped in poverty and ignorance; too many talents blighted by lack of opportunity; too many men and women who never achieve their full potential; racial

and religious prejudice in the South and in the North; the invasion of personal freedom by government and by large organizations; juvenile delinquency and social disintegration in the big cities; corruption and the misuse of power; and creeping mediocrity in every phase of our national life. . . .

The establishment of a durable peace, the strengthening of a free society, the enrichment of the traditions on which freedom depends—these cannot be achieved by aimless or listless men.[8]

The stories given above are but a few of thousands which could be told to illustrate how women are working, in big ways and small, to use their compassion, their energies, their votes, and their combined economic power for the strengthening of society. Many are responding to basic social upheavals which occur as ancient cultures adjust to modern pressures; as mankind struggles with vast human problems of which, until recently, most people were hardly aware.

❀

Nine

Women in Groups

In discussing what it is that urges volunteers to devote their time, without pay, to helping others, Dr. Edward C. Lindeman, the adult educator, commented:

> The act of volunteering is an assertion of individual worth. The person who, of his own free will, decides to work on behalf of the good of his own community is in effect saying: "I have gifts and talents which are needed. I am a person who accepts responsibility, not because it is imposed on me but because I wish to be useful. My right to be thus used is a symbol of my personal dignity and worth." [1]

Caritas, charity, or love has been a dominant concept in many civilizations. It is part of the doctrine of most religions. How this concept has been carried out varies, but the roots go deep. Furthermore, "rain does not fall on one roof alone," says the proverb of the Cameroons. People are becoming aware that if everyone's conditions can be improved, they personally will be helped as well as their neighbors. They are realizing that if each person does one small part, wherever he may be, it is possible to raise the quality of life for all their children—maybe even for themselves as well.

Bradford Smith says:

> It is this habit of voluntary association, proliferated throughout the society, which makes the nation invulnerable to dictatorships and which provides a kind of chain-mail defense against any tyrannical group. The individual by himself is powerless. But as the member of an association he is strong.[2]

And Mahatma Gandhi is reported to have said: "I look upon the increase in the power of the state with the greatest fear, because, although while apparently doing good by minimizing exploitation, it does the greatest harm to mankind by destroying individuality, which lies at the root of all progress. . . . The conception of individual worth [is the] chief distinction between democracy and totalitarianism."

As we have seen, many women start to carry out useful work as individuals, but find they can accomplish more when they join with the energies of other people to supplement their efforts. This is one basic reason for organizations. Through them, people with similar purposes can unite, thus gaining strength.

As do men, great numbers of women belong to labor unions, church groups, professional organizations, parent-teacher groups, or co-operatives, using these (and other) channels to bring about desired change. This change may be reflected in new and better laws, new curricula, new safety measures, better race relations, or in many other ways. People are no longer always waiting for governments to make the first moves. Many are thinking and acting increasingly for themselves.

In his native Sweden, a year or two before his death, Dag Hammarskjöld spoke about all men and women who work outside their own narrow personal lives:

> The health and strength of a community depend on every citizen's feeling of solidarity with the other citizens, and on

his willingness, in the name of this solidarity, to shoulder his part of the burdens and responsibilities of the community. The same is, of course, true of humanity as a whole.[3]

Millions belong to women's organizations throughout the world.

Such groups form a training ground for citizenship. From the little village club to the powerful branch in some great city, from a gathering in a small church hall to a massive international conference, it is all part of the same huge job of work. The women involved learn about voting, including the grounds on which to select candidates; they become used to preparing reports, understanding both the implications and the omissions; they learn about funds and budgets; they become familiar with orderly procedures in the handling of business; their eyes are opened to the magnitude of needs throughout the world. Then, accustomed to thinking in wider terms, they combine their energies toward broader and broader goals. Many, at national levels, work to assist other lands.

The Catholic Women of Austria are an example. They have long been helping war-torn Korea. Over a period of many years they have organized a Family Fasting Day throughout the length and breadth of Austria. By this one means, they collect substantial amounts of money every year. What has this money done for Korea?

At the Port of Pohany, the Koreans have been able, thanks to these funds, to modernize their fishing activities, thereby helping the whole area to prosper. They bought a motorized fishing boat and new nets; more recently, an entire canning plant has been established, giving new employment to additional Koreans who now work not only in the actual fishing and in the plant, but also in distribution and selling.

Great areas of fertile land have also been bought with Austria's Fasting Day funds. These acres have been put into production for Korea's leper colonies, again yielding both food and employment for many people. A pilot farm has been established in order to teach young farmers to diversify their crops. They learn about pigs, poultry, cattle, and dairying. Young men from surrounding areas are brought in regularly so that they can take part in the training courses. The level of farming of the entire area has been improved. Still further use of the funds has included fellowships for Koreans, some held in Korea, and others in Austria.

No one will ever fully know what these efforts have meant to the young farmers, or to Korea itself. Yet it all started in the minds of the kindly women of another continent. Through them, individual Austrian families were encouraged to offer a day without food each year. The money saved by this abstinence was collected to help build a ravaged land thousands of miles from their own.

American women have not yet achieved full status in the working world, nor do they take part in the political world in proportion to their numbers. However, in their communities and in the nation they have made themselves felt out of all proportion to their numbers. They have done this primarily through their organized voluntary efforts. They come together in groups, combine their energies and give thousands of hours of their time to changing various conditions which they believe need to be improved. The time they have gained through modern housekeeping gadgets is devoted by many to improving their children's schools, working with voter education, or trying to improve race relations; they raise money for research in cancer or heart disease or infantile paralysis. Many of the progressive elements of the law—such as prison reforms—have been passed through their efforts and through the steady, relentless pressure and sponsorship of their vast organizations.

There are more than one hundred types of voluntary women's groups in the United States with countless branches all over the nation. These embrace a combined membership of something like thirty million women. The services that members give in hospitals and clinics, in playgrounds, school libraries and lunchrooms, would cost billions of dollars if the women had to be paid, or indeed, the services might not be available at all. Women do it because of their strong conviction that they owe a contribution to society beyond the one they make as wives and mothers.

"It is difficult to imagine what American life minus its volunteers would be like," said Dr. Lindeman. "They are to Democracy what circulation of the blood is to the organism."[4]

In his classic book *Democracy in America*, written as far back as 1835, Alexis de Tocqueville said,

> The most natural privilege of man, next to the right of acting for himself, is that of combining his exertions with those of his fellow creatures and of acting in common with them. The right of association therefore appears to me almost as inalienable in its nature as the right of personal liberty. No legislator can attack it without impairing the foundations of society.[5]

The extent of voluntary activity in the United States is, of course, associated partly with the high standard of living, the relatively short work week, and the availability of leisure time. But not entirely, for the idea of working with one's neighbor has always existed in this country. Partly it is a matter of national personality. There are temperaments that dislike being "lost" in groups. Neither the French nor the

Brazilians nor the Argentinians, for example, form readily into organizations to achieve their purposes. They prefer to work as individuals.

In Africa, on the other hand, men and women used to living in communal settlements and tribes feel the strength of interdependence, and work readily in groups and councils and organizations. Their folk-sayings transmit this philosophy: *Ofu ona aya hu n'aka* . . . "One bangle does not rattle," say the Nigerians; or again, *Onu kpokoma oghue ofifi* . . . "Only by pulling the muscles of the mouth together can one whistle."

In the United States the tradition of voluntary organizations started in the early frontier days. In a new country people worked for and with each other under conditions of great hardship without regard to sex or class or origin. They were establishing pioneer settlements. They freely offered each other protection and hospitality and care in the wilds or else they did not survive. Working together became a deep-rooted part of the American heritage. Women, improvising comforts as well as necessities in their cabins, made something vivid of real equality. In a country where there was obviously so much work to be done, respect for hard work of every kind became a tradition; so did the pooling of effort. There were quilting-bees when the women came together from far and near to sew one another's quilts; corn-husking was done almost as a festival, in groups; barns were "raised" and roofed by all the men from miles around who came together to build while the women made coffee and fed them all. No one was paid for this, but it was understood that when someone else was in need, you would be there to help with your tools and energy just as he had come to help you.

Another American tradition which leads to many voluntary groupings has been a basic desire to keep an eye on government, dating from the eighteenth century. "The least government is the best government," has long been a prevailing American view. Citizens' groups form rapidly even today over an issue where people feel the government is "stepping in" too much, or if they are not satisfied with what the government is doing. This may relate to any sort of question, large or small, local, national, or international. People may be concerned with a change in curriculum in their children's schools, or the location of a new highway; they may be demanding new laws to protect the rights of minority groups; local "watchdog" committees may form themselves to look into the way a town is spending its tax money; on the national level, groups organize voluntarily to pressure the government for (or perhaps against) aid to other countries, or to debate such matters as disarmament or financial support for the United Nations. The issues, big or small, draw to them individual citizens of any level who feel concerned and want to take action. By themselves, most people feel helpless. But banded together in groups, contributing resources and energy, withholding or giving support, boycotting or buying, voting "yes" or "no," men and women form an effective force. "If a centipede loses a leg it does not prevent him from walking," is an African recognition of the same truth: namely that there is strength and resilience in numbers. This is a widespread concept. People in many lands work freely together on a volunteer basis to achieve their purposes:

The people of Sambia, a village near Quito, in Ecuador, had to walk four hours a day to work in the capital city and four hours to return. . . . As they worked eight hours, that left them only time for sleep. Life was hard and cruel, but they had to go to Quito because only there could they earn a living.

The reason that it took so long was not the distance but there was a deep ravine. Climbing down to the bottom and up the other side was a wearisome and time-consuming part of the journey. They wanted to make a bridge, but the estimates of the materials that would be required and the cost made it absolutely impossible even to consider. Then came an engineer with a practical idea. The ravine ended right in the mountainside. If they could not build a bridge across the ravine, why shouldn't they tunnel into the mountain, then come out again on the other side of the chasm? This took no material; nothing but manpower, and this they had.

Three years they worked on it. Finally they had the tunnel going from one side of the ravine, into the mountain, then out on the other side of the ravine. It cost them nothing but great energy. Now to walk to Quito takes less than an hour a day. Already a bus runs to their village and their land has more than doubled in value. They are now able to sell their produce in the capital; the community has developed by leaps and bounds.[6]

In Greece the people of Bisdouni had a problem; their land dried so late in the spring that by the time they could plant, the crops could not ripen before the dry season set in. Thus, year after year, they would almost harvest a crop, but not quite. Again, by banding together, by giving of their work and energy for no pay, they were able to improve their lot. Men and women alike got out their shovels. They dug a canal and thus were able to drain and plant the land a few weeks earlier each spring. Within months after the work was undertaken, they had gained their first good crop.[7]

In England, the same kind of voluntary effort can be found:

There is nothing glamorous about dirty laundry, nor cooking, nor giving baths, nor cleaning houses. Yet the Women's Voluntary Services in England has a roster of thousands of women in towns and villages and hamlets all over Britain prepared to do this kind of humdrum task for their neighbors who may be old and helpless, or ill, or otherwise in need. No one pays a penny for these services. "It is nothing, I may need it myself someday," a Cockney housewife will tell you as she gets home after donating several hours of service.

The W.V.S. plan of "Meals on Wheels" makes it possible for thousands of people to remain securely in their own homes rather than going to some sort of institution temporarily or permanently when illness or trouble strikes. These same W.V.S. women turn out in cold and storm to feed fire-fighters, rescue crews, or flood victims. They sort and darn and mend, giving literally thousands of hours without pay and without rewards, other than the deep rewards of spirit.[8]

HOW ARE VOLUNTARY GROUPS NEEDED?

Whether in new countries or in industrialized nations, enormous needs exist, far beyond the capacities of any government to fulfill, whether these be measured in money, in trained personnel, or in commitment. They include:

Problems Related to Cities. Unemployment, overpopulation, school crowding, upheavals in moral values —such as prostitution, narcotics peddling, and delinquency in all its forms.

Problems concerned with Government. Informed citizens are needed in any free government to keep considering, discussing, examining, and speaking out on issues at every level of government.

Problems concerned with the world. As the world grows smaller, the developed countries have new and urgent responsibilities to increase their understanding and to share their trained personnel in order to help newer countries provide better standards and opportunities for their own people.

Matters of Spirit. All nations, old and new, share the need for constant thought and informed appraisal regarding the global questions of peace, disarmament, and spiritual strength.

TYPES OF ORGANIZATIONS

In some places, such as Ghana, Ceylon, or Indonesia, organizations tend to be highly centralized and semigovernmental in their financing, supervision, and control.

Elsewhere the group may be so independent that members keep splintering off because a minority would rather start their own group than accept a different plan or adopt a program preferred by the majority. As members find it hard to co-operate or submit, these groups keep dissolving, reforming, making little progress with the job they mean to do; they waste their energies through petty rivalries, jealousy, and bitterness.

Often the hierarchy system prevails. A few energetic dominating people hold office, and continue to hold it year after year. They have little trust in the capacities of their members so they do most of the work themselves, often feeling somewhat martyred about it. Often they are able people but they diminish their value by being self-righteous and superior.

Mrs. Important will tell you: "I don't want to, but I must remain President because there is no one else capable of taking the post."

How much chance has she ever given to anyone else to grow into the job, or how much responsibility has she been willing to share so that others might also learn? She likes being Mrs. Important, so she holds tight to the reins.

In many areas of the world, however, committee systems are usual. Officers are elected; there is rotation in office so that a maximum number of people have a chance at leadership; the work is divided into sub-committee responsibilities so that most members are given worthwhile work to do, in proportion to their growing abilities. Everyone likes to feel useful, no matter how simple the job may be. By dividing responsibilities, instead of holding them in the hands of a few, members get a sense of participation. Only when they feel a real part of the work will they remain vitally interested and active, and move from one level of skill to a higher one.

Belonging to a number of varied and free groups—family, job, church, the town council, a parent-teacher group, an adult education class, a fire company, a farm co-operative—whatever the groups may be—stimulates a person to become aware of human variety. Not everyone thinks as he does. This raises healthy questions in his mind about his own attitudes and keeps him from growing rigid. As he shifts from one group to another, he wonders, thinks, questions—and therefore grows.

By no means everybody wants to give his time for other people. Many are not convinced that they have any responsibilities whatsoever beyond those of their immediate family. Others make a try or two at contributing in some way to the common good, but somehow cannot find the way.

When Begum Liaquat Ali Khan was the Ambassador to the Netherlands from Pakistan, she examined what makes it difficult for some citizens to offer their energy for their nations. In addressing the Tenth International Conference of Social

Work in Rome in 1961, she listed a number of "gaps" where understanding often breaks down, so that barriers and resistance arise. She suggested that "gaps" occur frequently between:

Government and people.
Leaders and workers.
Professionals and nonprofessionals.
Rich and poor.
Intelligentsia and the masses.
Old and young.
Planners and planned-for.
Thinkers and doers.

She said, "Each tends to live within jealously guarded boundaries; to preserve and often to 'fossilize' its identity; to create and [lock itself safely into] special watertight compartments. This cannot and should not be so."[9]

Voluntary groups can, if they choose to work at it, bring about many kinds of change which help a nation to grow in strength. For example they can:

Encourage people's sense of understanding, responsibility, and co-operation through adult education and work with schools.

Hold educational, cultural, and health programs in cities and rural areas. By reaching deep into the citizenry by house-to-house canvasses, conferences, seminars, and classes, they can help to raise standards of daily living.

Work with lawmakers and the laws, so as to open new opportunities and help protect people's rights—all people's.

Develop economic outlets, vocational training, cooperatives, and other means through which people's capacity to learn can be increased or shifted, thus helping to raise incomes and strengthen economies.

Enrich communities by helping to carry out the day-to-day needs of institutions which are vital in a community but are usually struggling for life—such as hospitals, schools, museums, libraries—where shortages of both personnel and funds are often crippling.

No one would want to lay down rules for any organization. No two are—nor should they be—exactly alike. Each must be flexible enough to respond to new ideas, to the interplay of its own members, and to new experiments. But among the useful functions of well-organized clubs are the ways in which they help men and women to realize that in cooperating they gain strength; they also learn to accept a majority decision; their horizons of interest and understanding are broadened beyond the limits of their own personal lives.

To contribute effectively, voluntary groups must have that stability which comes from being well-organized and well-led. If they have good and understanding relations with the government, with professionals in their field, and with those who are volunteers, they have enormous potential strength.

Ten

How Do Women's Organizations Work?

WE HAVE SAID there is no set pattern to the way women's organizations work. Much depends on the purpose of the group:

Is it mostly for companionship and sociability?

Is it seriously for the purpose of learning, with a plan and sequence to it?

Is it for cultural pleasure in one of the arts or another?

Have its members come together for a specific job, such as helping with a political campaign, sewing for a hospital, or raising funds for a school?

Does the Board actually run some institution? If so, do the members really work or only talk?

Does the group exist purely to give status to Mrs. Important, whom no one dares defy?

It is good to be clear in one's mind about one's own organization or club. Knowing that in different circumstances there will be different answers, there are several questions which all groups might ask themselves from time to time:

1. Exactly what is our group really trying to achieve?
2. Within the past six months (or year) what real steps have we taken in that direction?

3. Has most of our membership been encouraged to express itself and take part, or have a few people done this and everyone else been silent?
4. Should our group remain purely a woman's group or would we fill our purpose better if we were working more closely with men?
5. Is our group broadly representative or would it be stronger if it included more people from other races, classes, religions, nations, castes, economic levels, ages?
6. If it did, would we still find unity and common purposes?
7. Would we be more effective in the community if we were less exclusive? Might we perhaps understand the community's problems better if we saw them from more points of view?
8. On what *is* our membership actually based?

   Is it:

   social position

   wealth

   husbands' jobs (army wives, college faculty, and the like)

   an experience in common (alumnae groups, garden club, members of an orchestra)

   common concern about a problem, or common interest in a subject (discussion group, town zoning, marriage law reform)

   where we happen to live (community social groups, neighborhood clubs)

   interest in a particular institution (hospital, church, school)

   professional bond (group of journalists, lawyers, youth workers)

9. Is our membership a mixture of the above? If so, how do we decide who is let in and who is not?
10. Are young people included? Are they responding? Do they feel comfortable with us, and part of us, or do they sit quietly as mere observers? Have they any true voice in the proceedings? Does anyone really listen to them and do we ever take any of their suggestions? Are the young people interested? If not, why not?

Though purposes vary, size of group varies, type of membership varies, there are nevertheless certain problems that most groups face in common whether they are meeting in Frankfurt, Santiago, Denver, or Seoul. Basic problems are the same whether the members wear cheongsams, turbans, or tweeds.

FUNDS

This is a fundamental and engrossing problem for nearly every group. However, despite the vital importance of raising funds, it should never be forgotten that money is only a means to an end. A group which is primarily engrossed in raising money is not using the spirits, brains, imagination and energies of its members to the fullest capacity. Fund raising rarely brings out people's deepest, best, and most creative inner resources—it is out of proportion if it takes up the bulk of everyone's thought and time.

Some people think government support (usually accompanied by government control, or at least supervision) is the most efficient way to achieve financial security. Sometimes there is no alternative, but this method is not always as easy as it looks.

> The women's organizations in Japan [writes a woman who has been active in them for years], particularly those whose

membership is in the millions, are an indispensable source for votes at election time. To legalize the government's gift of money to these groups, the law was changed so that local governments, through their social education sections, are authorized to give monetary help to various kinds of civic organizations, including women's.

Many times government officials have interfered with the programs of women's groups. Some cannot invite the kind of lecturers they choose because the government considers them too progressive; even in the choice of club officers the government officials have a great deal to say.

In prewar days, Japanese women were led by men and did as they were told without using their own initiative. They are still apt to obey orders, especially from government authorities.

Furthermore, the Japanese people have the custom to give "return" gifts. For instance, when A is given a gift by B, it is the custom that A should give a gift in return. When A becomes ill, and his friends bring gifts, he is supposed to give return gifts when he recovers. When someone dies, monetary offerings are given, but the bereaved family is expected to return half the sum in goods. This centuries-old custom is carried into the way of thinking of the Japanese people. Therefore women take it for granted that any monetary gift given to their organizations must be returned in the form of "obedience" or "votes" at the time of election.

This is not true with all women's organizations, but the government does not give monetary assistance to those organizations whose members are so enlightened that they do not feel it necessary to return anything.

Here is one of the big problems facing women's organizations. In this way some have already lost independence and become tools of the government.[1]

This situation is true not only in Japan but in its varied way throughout much of the world. It means that any group taking money from the government should do so with a clear awareness of all the possible consequences.

In countries where governments change rapidly, there is another danger for organizations which depend too heavily on government funds. Anything such as a clinic or school which was started under one government may have a hard time in getting funds from the next one. Frequently the attitude is, "We did not start it; why should we continue it?"

Some groups prefer to have less money but more freedom. In one of Indonesia's remote *kampongs* a maternity clinic was built with no government help at all. The women put aside a small half measure of rice each time they cooked the family's meal. Once or twice a week they took their little cupful to a large container in the main compound. When enough had been collected to fill the container, it was sold, and the money put aside for the clinic. Then it was slowly refilled again.

Imagine the dance and flowers and festival air when the clinic finally became a reality! It belonged deeply and personally to the whole village; they used it well.

The idea that the poor have nothing to contribute is widespread, but it is not true. Many assume that everything must be done for them free. This is a demoralizing idea. In fact, the world's poor have a great deal to offer. They cannot give money, but they can give time, and simple skills, and knowledge of their environment. Many of them would rather contribute what they can than be the objects of charity. There are many ways in which either a government or an organization can make it possible for people to exchange their idle time for items they need in order to raise their standard of living. Often they can be given the choice of paying for land, food, medical care or other services in either money or labor, depending upon their own free choice. This opens possibilities to vast numbers of people to share in a better life without being objects of charity, even when they have no money.

In New England (U.S.A.) it has long been possible for men to pay off their local taxes by contributing days of work on the roads instead of cash.

In Greece farmers were allowed to secure the services of a fine boar if they contributed a baby pig in repayment.

In Korea an improved type of rice was made widely available on the agreement that when harvested, the families would exchange some with their neighbors for ordinary rice. In this way they ate the ordinary rice, but made better seed available for others to plant. In a few years the whole area was growing the better rice.

In the Eastern Mediterranean a peasant farmer was asked if he would be willing to work ten days a year, during his idle time, on some community improvement such as roads or schools, if in return he were paid not in money but in a credit plan with a hospital to be used in time of sickness. He replied that there was not one peasant in the whole nation who would not jump at an opportunity to give his time and labor, which he possesses in abundance, in return for something so difficult for him to secure as hospital care.

In India the Salvation Army finds that even the poorest women, who have absolutely nothing themselves, will work to help others and get joy from it. Four babies in one particular Salvation Army orphanage in India are supported entirely by the women of two parched, poverty-stricken villages who sell firewood to earn money for "their" children.

There is gain whenever one can add to people's sense of

dignity by giving them a chance to contribute rather than always being objects of pity. Pity destroys the soul.

There are other ways besides government grants or laborious personal fund-raising, or exchanges of goods and labor, by which community action can be financed.

A businesswoman from Chile suggests: "We must begin to create the conscience of saving money among our people."

Saving money is always difficult. Living costs continue to go up and up wherever one lives; meanwhile the desires of people throughout the world are also increasing. They want education for their children; or a tractor, or a bicycle. Most people do not save easily. If they do put something aside, few give it away with any readiness. And yet, wherever people can be persuaded to pool their resources, each giving a small sum, much can be accomplished.

No one can force this kind of giving; it must come from within. But when the climate of opinion in any country arrives at the point when people *assume* that everyone will share in the responsibilities of his community according to his means, then there develops a strong civic force within the land.

RELATIONS OF NATIONAL GROUPS TO GOVERNMENT AND BRANCHES

It is natural that groups of citizens should work together with their governments on those actions which strengthen a nation. How this relationship develops depends in large measure on the type of government there is, the relative amount of state control or free enterprise; how much voice the people have in the selection of their own national officials; the economic level of the country, the skill of the organization's leader, and a range of other factors.

In March 1962, the heads of a number of women's international groups met together in New York to discuss their relations to each other, and to talk about some problems common to them all.

One part of their discussion centered around "What makes *voluntary* organizations important and different from government agencies and institutions? What needs to be carefully safeguarded if the voluntary aspect is to be maintained?"

Among the points they raised as being crucial elements of free institutions were:

Freedom of members to join and resign.
Freedom of members to express themselves.
Freedom of members to determine policy and program.
Freedom of members to pioneer and experiment.
Freedom of members to develop as individuals.

The group was well aware how necessary it is for organizations to co-operate with governments on specific projects and activities but pointed out that circumstances could arise in this relationship that would threaten the independent and voluntary character of the private group, as for example:

Government decree or law requiring inspection of the group's administration.
Apathy of the group or the public towards government interference.
Too great a reliance on government funds.

"There is need for continuous vigilance," they reported, "on the part of voluntary organizations in their relations with governments . . . to safeguard:

Their right to formulate purpose, objectives, programs, contributions, and procedures.
Their freedom to recruit members and staff.

Their possibilities to expand and to extend their activities.

Their right of associating with other organizations, nationally and internationally.

The privilege of withdrawing from an agreement with government if changed circumstances so warrant.

If these rights are safeguarded, they believed, organizations remain free.[2]

Where groups operate, as many do, in an orderly way from local to state to national levels, then the national leaders are generally experienced and work relatively smoothly with the government.

Marjorie Tait writes of the National Council of Women of Britain:

> Information is constantly going out to the nation-wide network, and constantly flowing back from the branches. When a Bill which concerns women in any way is laid before Parliament, it is, of course, closely considered; and if there are any points on which it is thought urgent that the Bill be amended, the branches are asked to approach their Members of Parliament before the Second Reading.[3]

She outlines the four functions of the National Council of Women of Britain, which are, of course, similar to those of many other national groups, but which indicate the close relationship there can be between government and voluntary groups:

> [The National Council] acts on occasion as a *pressure group* on the Government. It also uses its machinery of *consultation* to collect information for the Government, for example, in giving evidence before a Royal Commission. It is an *educational agency*, a training ground for public affairs; and a *coordinating body* for local interests and for special interests.[4]

Leagues of Women Voters in the United States, Philippines, Singapore, and other countries, the Frederika Bremer Association of Germany, and many other national organizations have a close concern with governmental affairs and a dedication to help women understand the issues of their country so that they can make responsible decisions.

In many countries women's groups are organized with widespread branches which extend out into the furthest corners of the nation, able to reflect the opinions and desires of their members.

C.I.F. (*Il Centro Italiano Fémminile*) is a good example of the way this works in many organizations.

C.I.F. is one of the important, influential, and widespread women's organizations of Italy. There are twenty-five provincial branches with headquarters in the principal cities of Italy; under their supervision are approximately five thousand local groups in smaller communities, reaching to the level of the most modest householder.

In addition, there are other organizations, both local and national, some with international ties, affiliated with C.I.F. These groups maintain their own autonomy and character but join with C.I.F. when their interests lie in common, making of the whole a truly flexible federation.

Sometimes this flow from local housewife to National President, and through her to international levels is, as we have seen, clear and effective. When organizations are well led, they provide a channel through which the lowliest *villagers* can know they have a voice in their own affairs; the *women* of the organization can know they have government and often international support; the *government* can know that it may call on the women of the country to work for its objectives at the level of the local community, which is where progress must actually take place.

Sometimes, however, the views of the people on the local level are ignored, being considered unimportant. Autocratic individuals at state or national levels can decide that "they know best." They sometimes make decisions to suit themselves, not really reflecting the local viewpoints. Local groups must watch to see that this does not occur.

Relationships between organizations and governments are not always co-operative. Majority views, consensus of opinion, the vote of the Board, or well-expressed public desire, can all be ignored if these do not agree with the ruling intent. Some governments can dissolve an organization at will with the stroke of a pen, and set up their own puppet group which will carry out the prevailing political intent with less public voice or participation.

People often agree that this is bad, but they shrug their shoulders and say, "That is the way it is. What can you do?" Perhaps the only thing you can do is to make sure that everyone clearly understands exactly what has happened and why. Evil often fades under the bright light of public exposure.

HOW CAN WOMEN MAKE THEIR ORGANIZATIONS MORE EFFECTIVE? Twenty-one United Nations delegates discussed this question together in 1960. In addition to the United States they represented: Australia, Burma, Canada, Chile, Denmark, El Salvador, Finland, Ghana, Greece, Guatemala, Israel, Pakistan, Poland, and the United Kingdom—a truly broad sampling of many cultures, attitudes, and experience.

They emphatically agreed that women's organizations should work more effectively. They should "rethink their combined abilities" the delegates suggested, each group looking at itself in relation to its own country and asking itself such questions as:

How can we best help—would it be in the fields of education, legal rights, or perhaps greater support of professions, such as nursing?

Are we continuing in traditional lines of work without looking to see if these are still the most needed?

Are we using our members' particular skills to their best advantage?

Then, they said, each group should consider carefully what it is "prepared, competent, and willing to do." On that basis they should draw up a long-term plan, in some detail; if necessary encourage their government to give technical assistance; *then stick with it.*

"Too many groups scatter themselves over so wide a horizon that they do nothing really well," they said. "Or, under one set of officers they start something and under the next they shift their plan. More might be accomplished if they did not try to cover so much ground, but went more carefully and deeply into fewer projects."

In summary the steps they proposed were:

1. Vision.
2. A careful appraisal of the needs.
3. A long-range plan, based on this appraisal, but suited also to the resources available within their group, resources measured in terms of:
   a. Ability.
   b. Time.
   c. Interest.
   d. Continuity.

"Only so," they agreed, "can women's organizations be counted on; only so will they make substantial contributions to their national growth."[5]

In speaking to the women of Pakistan, Begum Liaquat Ali Khan touched on the questions of "vision" and "appraisal" as they applied not only to her country but to much of the world. She stressed the imperative need for more work with rural areas.

"Until we can reach out to the village women and their families in a much . . . bigger way, we are but touching the fringe of our problems,"[6] she said.

RELATIONS BETWEEN PROFESSIONALS AND VOLUNTEERS

Unless there is a trusting and co-operative partnership between professionals and volunteers within an organization there can be much unhappiness. Professional workers can advise, direct and do the professional aspects of the job, but the volunteer is also critically needed to extend the services of the all-too-few professionals who cannot be everywhere; furthermore she has a particular role in policy-making, and in creating a climate of opinion in which problems can be solved.

Where frictions occur these usually stem either from the professionals feeling superior to the volunteers and "bossing" them; or the volunteers feeling superior to the professionals, considering them as "paid help" and treating them as inferiors. Frequently each group feels superior to the other.

What is important for both to understand fully is that neither can operate to her fullest value without the other; each supplements the other's work. The job of each needs to be clearly defined and each one's position both seen and respected. To keep the harmonies between both, it is advisable that there be frequent opportunities for them to talk together outside the setting of a formal meeting. But frictions do nearly always arise. To avoid these growing into real problems there needs to be:

A genuine desire on both parts to assist and understand the other.
A realization that neither is "superior"—both are important and both have distinct roles to play.
Easy opportunity to talk out any problems before they grow to big aggravations.
Adequate training for the volunteer as well as the professional.
Clear definition of responsibilities of each.

JEALOUSY AND RIVALRY AMONG MEMBERS

The twin sisters of Jealousy and Rivalry waste more time, destroy more good intentions, make more unhappiness, lose more good workers, than makes any sense at all. This is true from one side of the world to the other.

"If Mrs. X is elected President, I shall resign and start a new group."
"Who does she think she is, acting as if she knows about Health Clinics? My husband is Chief of Medicine. I should be on that Board, and not Mrs. Y."
"Work together on the hostel? Our group started first. Who would be President if we combined? They would never work under Mrs. X and we certainly would not want to work under *their* President. Besides, they want their hostel for working girls, and we want ours for students."

Those who destroy themselves and others from jealousy, do so because their focus is in the wrong place. They have lost sight of the job that needs doing. Instead, their own prestige, their status (or that of their husband), their own hurt pride, their own personal likes and dislikes fill their horizons. When the focus is right, it does not matter whether

Mrs. X and Mrs. Y are on a level of social equality or not, nor what their husbands do. Then rivalries fade over another club having the same purpose, like the hostel. The job and the need come first.

When two groups can co-operate and form their plans together there are more workers, less duplication in fund-raising, and more energy brought to bear on the problem; therefore it can often be solved more readily. One's position and identity are not necessarily lost when one co-operates; quite often both groups gain.

The Chinese book of Taoist philosophy, said to be about 2500 years old, contains advice which shows that jealousy and the desire for prestige are ancient human failings. Tao philosophy says,

The highest motive is to be like water; water is essential to all life, yet it does not demand a fee or proclaim its importance. Rather it flows humbly to the next level.

Nothing in the world is weaker or more yielding than water. Yet nothing is its equal in wearing away the hard and the strong. Thus the flexible can overcome the rigid. The whole world can perceive this but does not put it into practice.

Eleven

What About Youth?

As she grows up, every woman dreams of making a serene, happy home for a future husband and of bringing up children to their fullest capacities.

With life so different from that of their own youth, how can women guide their children—especially teen-agers—through the problems of today? Why is it so much harder than it used to be? There are a number of reasons:

1. The deep-seated changes of the world are creating enormous gulfs between conservative parents and modern-minded young.
2. In many parts of the world, young people are maturing sexually earlier than did their parents and grandparents; sexual maturity, however, does not always come in step with emotional and social maturity.
3. Knowledge is being extended so fast, science is advancing so rapidly that school books are quickly out of date. New viewpoints make many teachers and parents appear "old-fashioned" to the young.
4. Because there is increasingly so much to know in every field, there is a trend towards early specializa-

tion, which often leaves the student one-sided, ill-equipped to understand complex situations. Take the young science student, for example, who, deep in his laboratories, often learns little of human relations or the perspective of history or the wisdom of ancient philosophies.

5. Distance is shrinking. The world is moving closer together; increased tensions and competitions are acutely felt.
6. Specialized vocational training, automation, changing labor conditions, new bureaucracies all make flexibility in occupations more difficult. It is hard for youth to find his way, to choose, to shift to something else if he feels he has not chosen wisely.

Youth is seeking, copying, dissolving old ties, forming new ones, not necessarily those of which his parents approve. His own age group seems to influence him more than do either his parents or his teachers; this is often a source of dismay to parents. Old traditions seem to be thrown out of the window. Often the young person himself is pulled in opposite directions, not knowing what kind of a person he is or really wants to be, nor whom he wants to follow. Young people keep acting in ways that parents find hard because they, too, are unprepared to meet these difficulties. Their world, too, is in a state of confusion. Each is frequently out of step with the other, uncertain and perplexed.

How can the transition be made easier for both generations? Much of the difficulty lies in attitudes. If both generations can confer as equals on at least some points, this tends to draw them together.

Most young people are interested in talking with their

parents about basic matters that affect them all, such as the economic conditions of the family, whether the mother should work, the pros and cons of the political scene, taxes, and such subjects which were once considered "unsuitable" for youth. As young people feel their point of view respected, they tend to be less defensive and more a part of the family, even when the gulf between generations has been wide. If the young person feels his parents are also trying to learn and adjust and understand, he will tend to become easier himself. The quality of "respect" seems to be changing from old-time subservience to modern give-and-take.

Relationships between the generations are also likely to be more harmonious if both parents and their children can embark on absorbing activities together at home. A sense of shared challenge brings satisfaction to both groups. Most farm families who regularly work together understand each other quite well. For urban families, the joint challenges must often be planned. They may be found in learning a language or mastering a violin together; in mountain climbing or building a boat together; in tailoring a suit or being joint hosts to overseas guests from unfamiliar lands. It does not matter what families do together so long as parent and child can learn and work and struggle together on some project *as equals*, not always in the relation of teacher and pupil.

More than a dozen parent-child combinations, for example, play among the fifty or so members of a community orchestra in Shaker Heights, Ohio. About half the orchestra are housewives and working women; a quarter are teen-agers; and a quarter are men.

It is not unusual in such an orchestra for a bank president to play second fiddle to a young school teacher, or for the brass section to consist of a teen-ager, a housewife, a football coach, and a chemical engineer. Harmony, the task at hand, quickly overrides any social, business, or age differences.

Free choice used not to be a part of children's lives, but in today's world, every adult is faced with a constant series of important choices and decisions. Wise choices, ones which are based on sound standards and careful reflection, cannot be learned overnight. They need to be experimented with and practiced, both in school and at home, throughout the growing years if wise and thoughtful choices are to be made in later years.

The sense of being trusted is probably the key to today's youth. When treated as equals, most young people will act as equals, but they resent being held back and "babied."

Greater responsibility, more free choice, less authoritarian handling is part of the answer in helping today's restless and perplexed young people. This does not mean license, or a breakdown of standards, or a lowering of expectations. Instead, it means even greater expectations on the part of parents.

Many of today's young people are ready for responsibility extraordinarily early, although superficially they may not seem to be.

A twenty-four-year-old boy from Berlin was on a student ship one summer. He was to be in the United States for only three weeks.

"Why so short a visit?" he was asked.

"I'm just coming for one purpose," he answered. "I have been invited to read a paper about my researches before the Congress of World Physicists, which is meeting in Philadelphia."

On the same ship was a young French girl whose tight skirt was always above her knees; she was rarely seen without a cigarette holder dangling from her languid hand. Her hair was heavily lacquered. Despite this "playgirl" appearance, she had won a top scholarship in world competition, and was headed for one of the most difficult electrical engineering courses offered anywhere—a course in advanced electrical computers.

Throughout the world the 4-H Clubs have proved how well high expectations work with thousands of farmers, both boys and girls. These young people conduct their own meetings, plan their own programs, keep abreast of developments in both agriculture and home economics. They rise to the responsibilities allowed them, and they do excellent work.

In La Union, Philippines, for example, the son of a small farmer planted 2 hectares of idle land with virginia leaf tobacco as his 4-H Club project. The year was good; he tended his crop well; it yielded over 4,000 pounds of high-grade leaf and brought the family 4,800 pesos.

When he went on to Agricultural College a few years later, his project had become the family's full support. He and his father worked it together most profitably.

Tens of thousands of children throughout the world never get to high school—or secondary school—or drop out partway because of the cost, or because they get restless and drift away to get a "pick-up" job, thereby condemning themselves forever to a life of poorly paid unskilled labor. This dropout problem has assumed grave proportions in the United States. One effort to attack it has been developed by the Co-operative Education Plan, part of the New York City Board of Education's program. They are gaining major successes because, like the 4-H Clubs, they ask more than usual of the young person, giving him more responsibility, treating him more as an adult. The New York *Times* reported this program as follows:

> [It is] one of the most realistic ways of bridging the gap from school to work for thousands of students each year, said Miss Brennan, Director of Cooperative Education. . . . Students participating . . . alternate between school and job during their junior and senior years of high school, taking academic subjects as well as job-related courses while they are in school. They are also rated by their employers on job performance and given school credit for satisfactory work ratings. Students are paired so that the job is covered at all times, with one student attending classes while the other is working. They compete in the labor market and receive prevailing wages. . . .
>
> Superintendent of Schools John J. Theobald pointed out that an outstanding asset of the program is its holding power and the goal of a high school diploma for scores of youngsters who might not achieve their objectives. Not only are we able to retain 99 per cent of our cooperative students until they complete their high school education, he said, but 80 per cent are kept on in permanent jobs after graduation. . . .[1]

In the search for companionship, in the hope of finding themselves, in the desire to find either excitement or purpose, youth tends to group itself into clubs or gangs, or organizations of one sort or another. Some of these are good and some are bad. Some are time-wasting and achieve nothing; others are politically biased; some are focused on community welfare or public service; some on sports; a small percentage focus on real damage and destruction.

One can divide youth movements into three kinds:

1. Those planned, created, and run by youth itself.
2. Those sponsored by concerned adults in the community.
3. Those sponsored by governments.

When a country is in crisis or ferment, youth groups, both students' and workers', often rise in rapid response. Governments have rocked under the impact of student pressure, as we have seen in Hungary, Korea, Turkey—to name a few.

Political parties throughout the world, aware of the "young vote," develop Youth Sections in their party structures. These can be valuable training grounds for intelligent participation in the affairs of the nation. In single party countries, they can be a useful channel for indoctrination, or they can be radical elements for extreme political agitation.

If today's young people are going to be involved in heady, exciting, meaningful activity outside the home, it is little wonder that they chafe and are restless under extreme parental authority.

Young people need adult guidance and wisdom, but they are less likely than in former years to be docile. Most of them want to throw their weight into the issues of the day. These need not necessarily be political, but must necessarily be real.

This is where parents and communities and organizations can help them. Youth wants to contribute. Much of it is burning with unspent energy, both mental and physical. If this energy is not channeled into adult, constructive, appealing, purposeful paths, it can be dissipated into inertia, or spend itself in hooliganism, or turn to alcohol, drugs, or sex. It most certainly can lead at the very least to restlessness and misunderstanding at home.

Many groups have shown great awareness of this need in the youth with whom they work. Where, for example, American Girl Scouts once were content to earn badges for personal skills and accomplishments in athletics or campcraft, the focus has now broadened considerably. Girl Scouts at young ages work in hospitals and recreation centers; they help at election periods; they plan and carry out projects for the children of migrant workers; they join with Girl Guides all over the world in international exchanges, competitions, and gatherings in order to help bridge barriers of race, nationality, culture, class, and religion. It is becoming more and more usual for young people's groups to set their own purpose in line with their country's needs for growth and development. These purposes seem real to the young people because they *are* real.

The Federation of Youth Clubs in Nigeria, for example, has expressed its major aims in terms of helping to draw together that great nation. Writes one of its leaders:

> Our purpose is to help boys and girls know and take an interest:
>
> 1. In one another, no matter whether they are Ibos, Hausas, Yorubas, or whether they are Christians, Mohammedans, or Pagans; or whether they are rich or poor.
> 2. In the area, town, or village where they live, to think well of the people among whom they live, no matter who they are, or what tribe they come from.[2]

Young people have much energy to throw into reconstruction (whether it be building or rebuilding); into the education of others; into the blending of ancient values with modern; into the development of natural resources and the breaking down of human barriers.

By no means all *want* to do so, however.

"My children come home for the school holidays," said a woman from India. "They drink Coca-Cola, play jazz records, play a little tennis sometimes, but that is all they do. And thousands like them all over our land are restless, bored, useless. What can we do?"

"Our generation had a great social conscience," said someone from Egypt, "but our children seem apathetic nowadays."

It is true that some have not yet seen themselves in a broad context, or are unable to act freely. Nevertheless, throughout the world, countless thousands of other young people *are* helping to move the world ahead.

The following examples show how some young people are using their time:

In Korea: *Medical students, aware of the rural needs, have organized themselves into teams during the summer holidays. They tour the remote countryside each year in traveling units, caring for the villagers.*

In Colombia, Bolivia, and elsewhere: *Senior high school and university students have their choice of serving in the military, or giving a year to teaching in the villages in order to help lower the high rates of illiteracy.*

In the United States: *Students concerned with discrimination against minorities formed a Northern Student Movement. They offer tutoring to high school students, mostly Negro, who, because of crowded schools, poor teachers, inadequate facilities, or second-class curriculum requirements, have little chance to go to college or to prepare themselves for any but the most menial jobs.*

During the summer, the college students get themselves jobs to pay their own expenses. They work as icemen, truck drivers, office workers, garage mechanics, so that they can offer their free time, in the evenings and on weekends, in giving academic help to high school students. They hold classes in boys' clubs, in churches, in neighborhood centers, wherever they are needed; they tutor individually all over the cities where they are working.

The movement has spread from a modest start in 1961, until now it has affiliated groups at sixty-five colleges and universities. Hundreds of students are involved, both as instructors and in the classes.

Work camps are another answer to the question, "What can young people do?" Teenagers help to build schools or homes; they help to pipe fresh water down from mountains, to dig irrigation ditches, plant windbreaks, teach in literacy courses, or do whatever is needed to help communities strengthen themselves. More than six thousand young people from a wide range of countries have worked in some three hundred camps set up by U.N.E.S.C.O. alone. Countless more are working under the auspices of other groups such as World Neighbors, the Literacy Campaign, the Quakers, and many others.

Pierre Martin, a teacher, described the group he worked with in North Africa in a work camp of the Service Civil International:

"There were twelve of us, nine young men and three girls, working together in an isolated but strikingly beautiful spot in the Kabyle Mountains in Algeria. There was Stephen, a Swiss student-teacher; Milo, an apprentice electrician from Southern France; Joe, a psychology student from New York; Oddvar, a farm boy from Norway; Adber, a Kabyle studying in Algiers; Ali, a young Arab; Philippe, a Moroccan student of architecture; Jean, a mechanic, and myself, a teacher from France. We slept in the largest tent. The three girls had the second tent: Mady, an English chemist; Claartje, who taught physical education in Holland; and Sylvette, a Parisian typist."[3]

YOUNG LEADERSHIP

"If a little tree grows in the shade of a larger tree, it will die small," says a West African proverb.

Young people like to lead themselves. Practice in organization and in leadership are valuable by-products developed by the multitudes of youth groups throughout the world. Some adult assistance will always be helpful. Youth needs to make its own programs, learn from its own mistakes, and feel its own sense of responsibility. Advice from adults? Yes. Warm interest? Yes. But close direction and supervision is no longer in tune with the times.

Once it was enough for women's organizations to have a Junior Membership, which meant that young girls could come to meetings, sit meekly silent, observing and listening respectfully until, often months later, they were old enough to join. Once it was enough to have another kind of Junior Membership, where the girls met separately with their own programs, but always under the close supervision, direction, and authority of older members, as a class meets under a teacher's watchful eye. Now more is needed. Generally speaking, girls are not much interested in women's clubs—certainly not under those terms. They are marrying early, or going into careers; when they do their community work, they prefer groups which include men. They are feeling a growing sense of their own worth, and they need the opportunity to put this to good use.

Young people have enormous capabilities if these are not only allowed to flower but are actually demanded. Excellence is the standard that challenges them. When much is expected of the young, they produce their best. We need to trust them and can expect much of them, for they have great capacity.

Youth faces an even more complicated world than that with which we struggle today. They need every possible chance to try their wings, to exercise free choice, to learn self-confidence. Today's adults must give them increasing leeway to learn from their own errors if they are to stand firm later in the bigger arena of this complex world.

Already more than one ambassador at the United Nations, dealing with major problems affecting the lives and destinies of thousands of people, has been under thirty years of age. We who are older must recognize the new pace, the earlier responsibilities, the need youth has for practice in making decisions; thus we can help to prepare our young for the decades ahead. In all too few years, the world will be in their hands.

Twelve

What Next?

THE KEY WORD of our time may well be "urgency." We all live closer and closer to one another; our national lives are ever more intricately tied together. It is impossible any longer to shut ourselves safely and tranquilly within our personal and familiar horizon, whatever this horizon may be:

> Perhaps it is simply the four walls of a woman's house.
>
> Perhaps it is the village or town where her husband works and her children meet their friends. Her neighbors and the town may form her total view; school and other local problems are the breadth of her world.
>
> Perhaps the focus reaches farther—a province, a state, a nation, with its broader problems of government, progress, and peace.

Perhaps a United Nations patriotism will be a commonplace for future generations. Loyalty to nations may be a passing stage which will gradually be left behind in favor of greater regional and world loyalties.

Dr. Arnold Toynbee, the British historian, has urged this:

> Unification is, in the atomic age, mankind's only alternative to mass suicide. From now on we must give our paramount

> loyalty to the human race as a whole, instead of to the particular fraction in which we happen to be born.[1]

Following the same train of thought, the late Dag Hammarskjöld told the Swedish Academy in 1957:

> Only those who do not want to see can deny that we are moving these days in the direction of a new community of nations, however far we may be from its full realization, however often we may seem to have chosen the wrong path, however numerous the setbacks and disappointments have been. Could it be otherwise, when no other road appears open out of the dangers a new era has created?[2]

Living in peace with our neighbors is not easy.

We are ignorant about each other, often frustrated, prejudiced.

We are provincial, feeling more comfortable with the familiar.

We are lazy. It is easier to "jog along" as we are than it is to make changes.

We like to feel someone else is inferior. It seems to be a human failing to feel it easier to bear poverty if someone else is poorer; to undergo hunger if another is even more hungry.

It is sentimental to feel that people of different nationalities will necessarily like each other, will feel good will and want to co-operate if they can merely be brought together. In our daily lives we often do not like people whom we understand well and meet often. International understanding is not simple. In fact, it is the most difficult of all human relationships. Local affairs can go on at a face-to-face level, with people you know directly or indirectly; national affairs are more complicated and more remote, but still they deal with like people. But relations between nations are carried on remotely, through structures hard to understand—governments, inter-governmental bodies, supra-governments.

Despite this, a web of personal relationships also covers the earth, and, although it is thinly spun, it is incalculably tough. Through multitudes of personal ties, women can make a strong international contribution. Women can be "growing points" in a nation. Those who have the power to perceive have the challenge of educating and informing others; they need also to act as spokesmen for the less articulate. To do this, they must keep closely in touch with other women. Great strength lies in union based on mutual respect for difference, a union which has been created for a shared and honorable aim. How can a sense of unity be developed?

Children can be encouraged to feel at home in the world by the books they read, the films they see, the people they meet, their leisure pursuits. These can be as simple but as expanding to their horizons as stamp-collecting or exchanging letters with other youth.

Women of professions or business can themselves correspond professionally with their counterparts in other lands.

Individuals having chance meetings with one another at conferences, in people's houses, on trains, etc., can either let the encounter die, or can choose to pursue the other's acquaintance and make of it a real bond—one more small link in a chain.

Members of organizations, churches, unions, and the like can override national boundaries by pursuing common interests with kindred spirits of other lands, co-operating on international work such as refugee support, student exchange, freedom-from-hunger campaigns, family planning, international hospitality, and child welfare.

Another area in which women can make a quiet contribution to a blending of nations lies in the matter of intermarriages between races. These are becoming more frequent with the opening and easing of communications between nations and races. The attitudes of mothers can help to make such marriages a visible and harmonious blending of cultures, or they can contribute to the family frictions and dislocations which sometimes occur.

A Chinese mother, whose daughter had just married an Australian, wrote:

> Neither set of parents attended the wedding. We all had to get used to the situation, but I have come to the conclusion that the world is a small place today; the world of tomorrow will see the melting down and consequent mixture of the various races, colors, and creeds.
>
> Women have, I think, a great contribution to make in their various capacities to bring about the realization of "One World," not by the artificial imposition of particular ideologies, but just by the simple fact of their role as the keeper of coming generations, to ensure their survival, which depends on enduring harmony and peace.
>
> Harmony and peace can only be brought about today, in my opinion, when the various peoples of the world merge into one another and emerge not as white, yellow, or black; as American, Russian, or Chinese, but as Human Beings, citizens of the world.[3]

Openness to experience, a quick readiness to respond to new ideas and to new people—these qualities are the opposite of being "mentally provincial." They may well be the most precious elements in a human's equipment for life today. Many people have had little experience in developing such flexibility, yet it is a quality for which our world has great need. This is an area where women can work. They can see that their children are "mentally international" and thus prepared for tomorrow's world; they can help their husbands; they can work on it themselves through the books they read, the people they choose as friends, the way they use their time.

Throughout this book we have seen something of the extent to which women at all levels, in all parts of the world, share common hopes, common struggles, common problems, common desires. No one is alone in what she is trying to do; no phase of the task is too small; nor is any place "too far away."

No matter where we live or who we are, each one of us is caught up in the self-same task—that of finding how to live harmoniously on this earth. There are no ready answers. The answers lie in working on them.

Barbara Ward, the distinguished English economist and writer, sums it all up when she says: "The twentieth century is designed for men and women who dare greatly and dream greatly and let their work catch up with their dreams."[4]

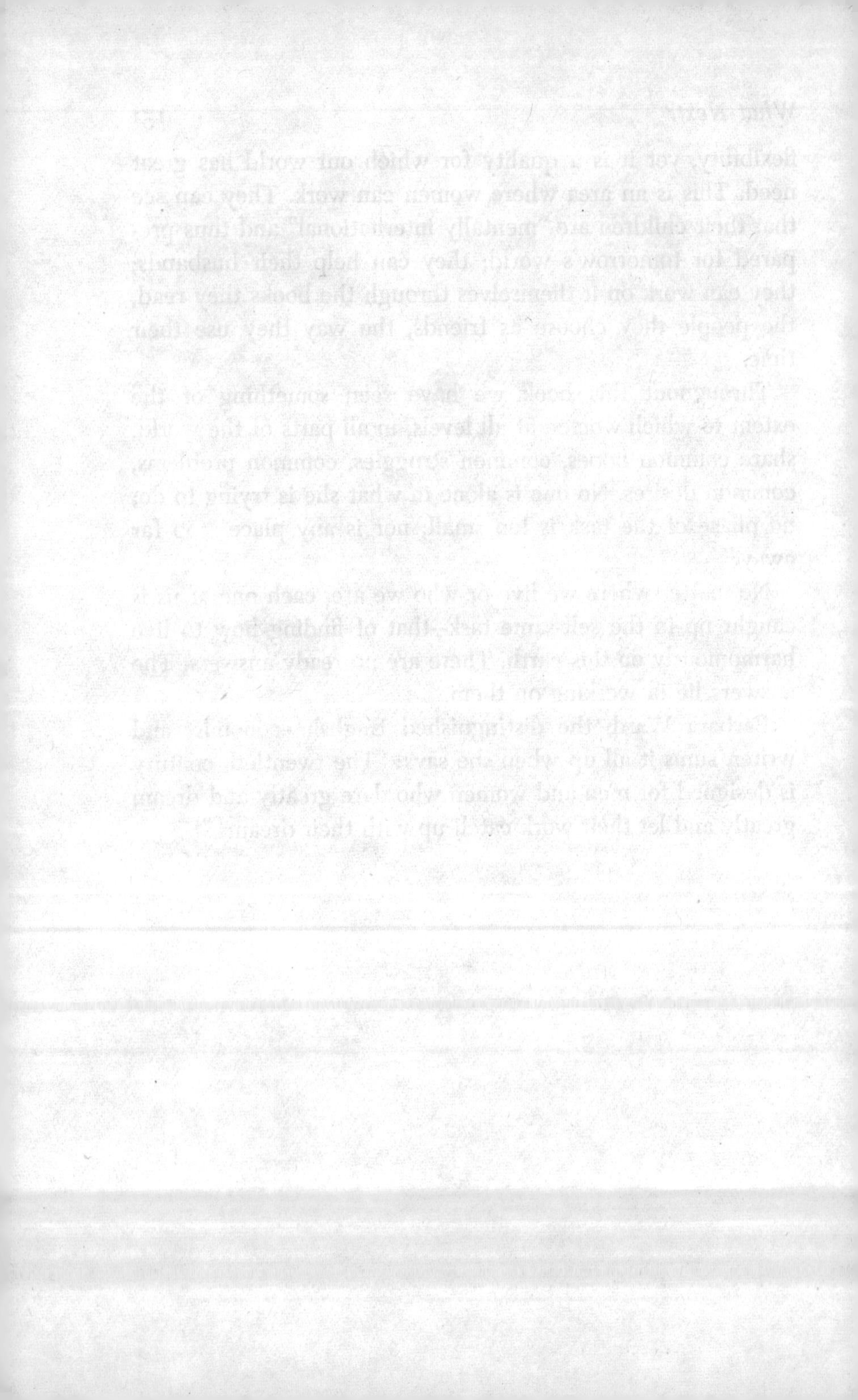

Part Two

How Do We Do It?

❁

What You Can Give

EACH OF YOU has three gifts to offer:

Your time.
Your energy.
Your abilities.

Part II of this book is arranged to help you make the best possible use of these gifts.

WHY DO PEOPLE GIVE FREELY OF THEIR TIME?

Many women find it hard to determine what, if anything, they might be doing in their communities. It may help to consider how other people choose their activities. What gets others started working outside their homes? Here are some of the pressures that push them:

A desire to be useful.
Need for money.
Desire to put their education and abilities to use.
Desire for interests outside the house.
Desire for new companionship.
Need for personal prestige.
Their husband's job requires them (*e.g.*, wife of the Mayor).

Whatever your personal and private reasons may be, you will find that outside activity can open a whole new world. On whatever level you choose to work, you will derive many satisfactions when you broaden your own horizons.

❀

What Needs to Be Done?

FIND OUT WHERE HELP IS NEEDED

Every locality has its own needs. Every group or individual has special abilities, interests, and resources. The first step is to fit the two together.

It might help you decide where you could be most useful if you consider some of the kinds of work being done around the world—jobs where women's thought, compassion, and energy make a real difference. Here are a few guidelines to help answer the question: "Am I investing my time where it can do the most good?"

BREAK DOWN BARRIERS

Women can help to develop situations which dissolve barriers, such as:

Race, class, tribal, regional, national differences.
The gap between generations.
The gap between rural and urban communities.

Some of the ways in which to bring diverse people together could be:

Invite participants from outlying towns, other economic levels, other races, other social groups, to take part in any conferences or classes you may be planning.

Plan joint activities for groups made up of all segments of society, with all groups represented in the *planning stages*, not just invited for the final event.

Set up special projects for children of different groups, such as camping trips, holiday outings, field days, or song contests.

Arrange special activities to bridge the gap between generations, such as "father-son" or "mother-daughter" game nights; banquets, song-fests.

IMPROVE CONDITIONS

Industrialization brings with it new problems for women. Countless areas cry for betterment:

Adequate day-care and nursery schools conveniently located so that mothers can work without concern about their children.

Increase in part-time employment for married women, so they can add to their incomes, but also be at home for part of each day.

Show employers that by dividing work, they gain flexibility of assignment, they can eliminate lunch hours, and thereby save in wages.

Residences and adequate housing are badly needed for working girls and students. Providing a roster of safe, inspected homes where girls could stay might be a quicker and more practicable approach than trying to build special residences—anyway at first.

Legislation related to working hours, holidays, and equal pay for women depends on the support of civic groups and the general public as well as of trade unions.

HELP TO EDUCATE

In addition to the obvious needs for more schools and teachers, more scholarships, more vocational training for adults as well as youth, there are other areas of education in which much remains to be done:

> The responsibility of voting often needs to be stressed and people educated to facts about issues that particularly need their careful votes.
>
> Better school curricula are needed in most countries—courses attuned to the twentieth century, though within the framework of each national heritage and culture.
>
> Millions of people need more information on health and nutrition. If you can take it where women are already gathered, such as waiting rooms of maternity clinics, so much the better. Short health films can sometimes be borrowed and shown at meetings, schools, or in the markets to help spread new ideas.
>
> To improve rural conditions, women can help by teaching new methods of food preservation, farming techniques, literacy. This requires going out into the villages and rural areas regularly and gaining the trust of the village women.
>
> Mass media, such as radio programs, newspaper columns, and plays can be used increasingly to help people learn of new developments, or to foster attitudes of self-help and community co-operation.
>
> More can be done in many areas to draw parents and teachers into closer relationship. Parents can often ease the teacher's path if they know and understand the problems at school; teachers can better help the children if they know the situations at home. Regular Parent-Teacher meetings, parties, or conferences, Parent-Days at school, Teacher Hospitality in homes can all be useful means for drawing the two groups closer to-

gether. Women, both as mothers and as teachers, have a real role to play in this.

If there were more women on Selection Boards concerned with qualifications and admission standards for scholarships and fellowships, more girls might be selected for such opportunities.

GET MORE VOLUNTEERS

They are needed in hospitals, clinics, feeding centers, libraries, museums, refugee centers, old people's homes, overcrowded schools. Here are some practical suggestions:

Set up a central file listing opportunities for service in the neighborhood so that people with time to offer can look over the needs and volunteer their skills.

Combine training programs among a number of institutions so that thorough basic instruction in standard volunteer practices can be given at regular intervals (later each institution can give its own volunteers localized instruction, but in this way much duplication can be avoided).

Work out joint community plans to make transportation, baby-sitting services, and other aids available so that more women can offer their leisure hours regularly.

WORK ON LAWS

Women can have a far-reaching effect by influencing the passage of laws. Study comes first.

What can be done to improve laws concerning marriage and divorce? Inheritance for women? Custody of children?

Does the money collected for local taxes benefit everybody, or is benefiting only special groups?

How are labor conditions and wages in your area? Are children working long hours? Are women workers sitting or standing? How is the light? Sanitation? Where and what do workers eat? Do they have rest periods?

Is there any legal protection for the poor, or do you need to establish a Legal Aid Society where the poor can get help when they are in trouble?

OTHER THINGS TO DO

Help the handicapped by teaching skills which will help them to be self-respecting and self-supporting.

Help newcomers—foreign students, businessmen, refugees—adjust to life in your community.

Assist in family-planning education programs.

Maintain your national heritage by preserving folk arts and crafts, recording songs and stories, acquainting children with the meaning of their nation's culture.

Naturally no one can choose for another the best outlet for her own energies. Each individual must respond to what she feels will best suit her interests and time, giving her a sense of fulfillment.

BUT: Once you have chosen the area of your own interest, stay with it; become good at it; learn it thoroughly if you want to be really useful.

THEN: Join others; don't duplicate effort. Who else in your locality is working along the same lines? Can you and your group supplement what is being done, rather than compete?

How to Go About It: The Individual

MEASURE YOUR RESOURCES

When deciding whether or not to take on a new project, how do you and your group rate on:

Ability: What kind have you? How much? How real is it?

Energy: Will a few people do everything, or is there a real supply of willing energy?

Knowledge: How thoroughly have you looked into the circumstances, facts, and figures? Do you have an informed understanding of the field in which you choose to work?

For example:

Are you excited about an orphanage when in reality there are only a few uncared-for orphans in the area? Might your energy be better used some other way?

Are you starting to raise funds for a residence or kindergarten or clinic when there are already three or four groups working for the same purpose? It sounds silly even to ask, but it happens.

Time: Be sure you estimate carefully how much time will be needed to see the whole project through, not just the first phase when people have initial enthusiasm. Will people give the time that is required?

Perseverance: Are you—individually or as a group—going to be able to carry through in spite of obstacles?

How strong are your working relationships with: other organizations in the community; government agencies; press, radio, and television personnel; professionals in your field? All or any of these may be important.

Your resources lie in yourselves. Are you analyzing them and using them to full capacity?

MAKE MORE TIME

How do women find time to participate actively in projects that interest them? There are three broad areas in which domestic life can be adjusted to encompass the demands of outside work:

Plan Ahead: Schedule your routine chores—shopping, meal preparation, housecleaning—to allow yourself more free time (and regular free time) for what you want to do.

Divide Responsibilities: Even from an early age, children can be helpful. Give them specific tasks to fit their ages. If they are proud of the work you are doing outside the home, the family will help you to achieve it.

Simplify: Reduce elaborate meals, fussy housekeeping. Keep entertaining unpretentious.

SHARE YOUR ENERGIES

Friends and neighbors can all benefit from joint ventures that provide relief from monotony and more time for everybody. Perhaps you can:

Take turns baby-sitting for each other, so that each of you has regular time off.

Develop car pools to ease the transportation problem.

Co-operate on food preparation and preservation; it is more fun and takes less total time if you work together and share the products.

Co-operate on laundry and marketing. This can also help to ease each other's loads.

PLAN YOUR OUTSIDE ACTIVITIES

What do you most want to accomplish? When you decide this, concentrate your time: many women dabble in a multitude of half-hearted interests.

Choose what you are able to handle without neglecting your family, for if they feel neglected, you soon will not be able to do anything.

No one can do all that she wants. The woman who really accomplishes decides what she feels to be her greatest interest, or the area in which she can best contribute. Does she like to write? To handle figures? To care for children? To teach in the villages? Then she puts her energies into that area regardless of:

What friends say.
Temptations to join other groups.
Flattery in other directions.
Summer heat, and a desire to go back to cooling drinks, mahjong, or bridge.

Even though it may not be their very first choice of interest, many mothers may wisely consider work that can be done:

At Home: telephoning; handcraft; typing; making things to sell; writing for the press; providing story hours for neighborhood children.

Near Home: hospital or clinic; day nursery; library; teaching; work in a food center.

GET OTHERS TO WORK

Where do you find people who will be willing to give of their own energy to help? Much depends on the purpose of your work, of course, but likely places to look are among other already-existent organizations:

Civic, religious, or cultural groups.
Social clubs.
Unions, industrial groups.
Farm co-operatives.
Students groups.

If your activity is going to affect everybody—work such as schools, hospitals, libraries, health activities, citizenship training, education regarding laws and rights, co-operatives—then it should include everybody. If not only the educated few but everyone has a voice in the plans, understands the problems, feels personally involved in the progress, then people at all levels of society will feel a pride and help to achieve the goal. Volunteers for such activities, therefore, should be drawn from all social levels and all economic levels. The work will go better, and will go deeper.

What about your friends? Of course, if you know people who share your enthusiasm, call upon them. But remember that a friend may feel she can take advantage of her acquaintance and not perform as well as someone else, or she may resent taking orders from you. Friends are, therefore, not always the best resource.

The key to effective volunteer activity should always be WITH and not FOR other people. Avoid the temptation to be Lady Bountiful. Nobody ever likes to accept charity, either mental or material.

HOW DO YOU PERSUADE PEOPLE?

Getting people to work without pay is no easy task anywhere. Each prospective volunteer must realize that she really is needed. Help her to see her place in the whole picture. Above all, let her know that her help is genuinely appreciated. Recruiting is a one-by-one process of persuasion; it is rarely successful by mass appeal.

Be ready for reluctance. Behind every hesitation there is apt to be some kind of fear. You may help to dispel it if you recognize the kinds.

Your timid recruit may be:

Afraid of seeming to neglect her family and of the criticism this might bring.
Shy of new people.
Feeling inadequate; afraid of appearing foolish.
Afraid her husband will not allow her to take part.

Some people are just not interested. Don't take time over them; they may get the idea later. Plenty of other people are interested. Here are some suggestions for helping women to overcome their fears:

Help them organize and plan their free time so they no longer worry about neglecting their families.

Instill in husbands a sense of pride in their wives' achievements.

Extend a warm welcome so that initial contacts are easier, to help the shy ones.

Give new volunteers short, varied assignments in order to build and hold their interest.

Provide training so they know what is expected and feel confident.

Give assignments to fit individual abilities and tastes. Not everybody is good at the same things.

Volunteers will stay with you and continue to work only if they feel that the work they are doing is really worthwhile. They will not do it for someone else's glory, or if they feel it to be senseless "busy" work. But if persuaded that their job is important, most will rise to responsibility.

Credit must be given freely where it is due. The successful leader builds people to their best selves. She does not let personal rivalries, jealousies, political differences, social status, or other irrelevant matters come between the volunteer and her value to the group. *Give members a voice in the plan.*

Would you want to work in an organization where you had no voice?

If volunteers are to feel the job important, they must feel that it takes special qualities to do it. That is why training is important. Not only does it improve skills, but it has real psychological effects on the volunteer.

A common weakness in most organizations is to plead with people to volunteer. However short-handed you are, you put yourself in a weak position if you approach people on the basis of "we need you," rather than taking the opposite position: "Here is an opportunity, but it is available only to people who are willing to take it seriously and really budget their time for it." Immediately you have created a different psychology in the potential volunteer.

If you plead with a person she has a sense of her own importance and power. She says to herself: "I will drop in and help them whenever it is convenient to me." If you make volunteers realize that you will take them only if they fulfill specified requirements of time and steadiness, then the approach becomes different. They say to themselves, "This is something I would be proud to be associated with if I can qualify and be accepted."

Training can be given in stages. This gives people a sense of moving ahead. Regardless of whether a woman is to be a member of the Board, or will address envelopes, or whatever role she is to play, everyone should be required to take a first stage of training which gives the organization's philosophy of work and its basic purposes. This helps each person to see herself in the total picture. No one should be exempt.

Then, to qualify for specific posts, there can be a second stage of training, probably longer and more detailed. As a part of this, the volunteer should be required to put in a certain number of working hours.

If such requirements are established, you can develop:

A pride in accomplishment.
A sense of belonging to a whole.
A recognition of personal progress, and a desire to become more and more skilled.
A means for dropping "dead wood" and undesirable elements who nearly always refuse to take training.

The American Red Cross offers a good example of how people respect and respond to strict requirements. Women take courses as much as one hundred hours in length in order to become "Gray Ladies" and help in hospitals; others take long sessions to become Nurses Aides, or Waterfront and

Lifesaving Instructors. People take them seriously, knowing that if they do not complete the requirements, no amount of wheedling or string-pulling will allow anyone to hold those volunteer jobs with the Red Cross.

The Junior League of America is another group aware of the value of strict requirements. Although the country's wealthiest and most socially prominent girls belong, each must take hours of training and must faithfully contribute a specified number of volunteer hours a month or she is dropped from the League. It does not matter how important her father is, or what excuses she may offer. She knows from the start that if she fails in the part she has agreed to do, she is letting down the administration, she is failing other people. So her sense of responsibility is enlisted.

As long as organizations let volunteers come and go at will, putting no demands on them but being grateful for any crumb of time or interest, the volunteers will remain as casual and irresponsible as many are today. Humans have a basic "need to be needed." One can build on this, but the need must be real.

TIPS ON TRAINING

Learning is often uncomfortable. It means reacting differently from the old comfortable ways. It requires motivation and will power, and some means for carrying out the desired action.

Generally you get action when you rouse self-confidence, understanding, and trust, acquainting your volunteer with your group's purposes and way of working. Whether training takes place in an organized class, at an interview, or on-the-job, here are some pointers:

Begin at the beginning: Because you are familiar with your subject, it is easy to assume that your audience is, too. What may seem simple and elementary to the expert may require careful and perhaps repeated explanation to the novice.

Tie new learning to old: New ideas are easier to put into operation if they can be related to something that is already known. Try to find frequent examples which make a bridge with familiar things.

Be satisfied with little changes: Progress is a series of nudges—not a big jump. We must be willing to take advance motion if it is in the right direction.

Get personal: Most people respond better to personalities rather than to abstract ideas. Even if it is an abstract idea that you are trying to get across, give it human warmth by using anecdotes or telling of past experiences in the area.

Don't expect too much too soon: Give your volunteers time to absorb—and apply—what has been presented. Be patient with slow progress.

Move people ahead as they demonstrate competence: There is no quicker way to lose a good volunteer than to keep her stuffing envelopes when she could be writing radio scripts. Use your volunteers to the height of their capacities; they will respond with even greater efforts.

❀

How to Go About It: The Organization

WHAT MAKES A GOOD MEETING?

A meeting fulfills its purpose if people can see that:

Progress is being made.
There is a plan for the future.
Each person is really important if the goals are to be reached.

Here are some guidelines that have universal application:

WHAT IS THE MEETING FOR?

Keep in mind the big picture. Sometimes regular meetings become so buried in minor details and reports that over-all purposes are lost. It helps to reassess these purposes at intervals. You may want to break the group up into small sections every few months just to discuss them. It is amazing how frequently people are not trying to reach the same goals, but do not know it. Naturally this causes friction. It is good to discover it early if it is happening. Even the best-intentioned group will come to a grinding halt if, without realizing it, some members are aiming at different targets. Try to:

Agree on goals.
Establish a timetable to achieve them.
Assign projects according to ability and interest.
Look for elements of discontent, listen until you understand them, then remove the causes.

KEEP IT LIVELY

Group discussion, debate, demonstrations, and films frequently hold audience interest better than lectures. Participation by the members usually promotes an atmosphere that stimulates them to thought rather than to sleep!

PLAN SEATING ARRANGEMENTS CAREFULLY

These are more important than you might think. If it is a group discussion, try to arrange the chairs in a circle or a Y shape, or a V. Make it easy for people to see one another's faces. The backs of people's heads do not stimulate, but faces do.

HELP PEOPLE GET TO KNOW EACH OTHER

Interesting experiences and backgrounds often remain unknown unless specific efforts are made to bring them to light. If the group is not too large, it is often possible to take time for introductions—not just names but something unexpected about each—"She plays the harp"; "she has seven children"; "her hobby is mathematics," etc. It is easier for people to introduce their neighbor than to introduce themselves—they feel less self-conscious. These introductions can be fun. Give each person a specific responsibility in the group:

Doing research on a needed subject.
Preparing progress reports on various stages of the work.
Welcoming and indoctrinating new members into the group.
Developing reading lists.

Arranging transportation and baby-sitting.
Recruiting or training volunteers.
Raising funds.
Helping with publicity.

DON'T GET BOGGED DOWN

From the beginning, keep track of your program as you move down the agenda. Is the whole group in touch with the subjects being discussed? Are ideas getting across?

Dorothy Height, an experienced Y.W.C.A. leader in New York, offers these questions that each leader might ask herself:

> What can be done to help everyone present to enter most fully into the experience and gain most from it?
>
> What do we, as a group, need? What do we bring to the group? Is our emphasis in the right place? Are we dealing with the right questions—that is, the questions of most concern to this particular group?
>
> What will each person be able to do when she goes home? Are the meetings influencing attitudes, behavior, and the willingness to work?

Each person should react with a desire to know more. When she asks herself (rather than the teacher) what she is learning, then real progress has been achieved.

If, at the close of a meeting, each member of the group goes home clear in her mind about the next step—and her own personal responsibility in accomplishing it—then the meeting has fulfilled its purpose well.

WHAT ARE THEY THINKING?

How do you sense satisfaction or disquiet in the minds of your group?

Provide a climate of freedom where people are not afraid

to air their views. This means everyone, not just your friends, or those who speak out easily, or those who are socially prominent. Make the shy and the young and the new feel at ease also, so that each member gives her opinion freely. Let her know she will be listened to, and her ideas considered, whether finally acted upon or not. Whispering in the background is a sign that people are unwilling or afraid to speak openly. It should be a danger signal to the leader.

How can you make people feel free to speak?

By sincerely wanting to know what is on their minds. The sincerity comes through. If you listen, you may find you have to change carefully worked-out plans because they are not filling the needs of your group. You have to listen with your inner ear, weighing carefully what people say.

If a leader does her job well, each participant will leave the meeting with a sense of purpose; each will feel that she herself is involved. If they do not, the leader should search herself, not blame the group.

CHANGE OF PACE: DON'T LOSE PEOPLE FROM BOREDOM[1]

Audiences in many lands are getting restless. You can tell by the amount they shift their position during a speech! A restless audience is a captive audience.

Why?

People are less willing than once they were to be dominated by experts.

The Answer:

Use the experience and abilities within your group more fully. People have more ideas and more to offer than you may suspect. Use them! Give them a chance!

How?

There are a number of ways:

PANELS

A panel should be chosen from those who know the subject; three members is usually plenty; six is an absolute maximum. They should be people who talk easily and clearly.

The moderator opens the session by a brief preparatory statement about the topic, then throws to the panel a good, controversial question on the subject.

The panel picks up the subject, discusses, asks additional questions of one another, expands or debates a point, carries on the give-and-take of a conversation; what they say is informal, unrehearsed, unwritten.

To make this work well, panel members need to do one thing in advance. They need to decide in general—not in detail—what points each will cover. In this way, the discussion gets somewhere—it will not be aimless. But don't plan details of what each will say. The purpose of a panel is *to explore a subject*, not give speeches.

At the appropriate point, the chairman opens the session to questions (not speeches) from the floor so that everyone who wants to can join in.

SYMPOSIUM

A symposium is different; it is made up of short prepared speeches of not more than seven to ten minutes each. Each speaker develops a different aspect of the same subject—he or she takes just a few points, presents them clearly and vividly, then sits down to let the next speaker develop the next phase of the subject.

The change of voice and personality keeps the attention of the audience better than a single long speech on the same subject; furthermore, it brings together several points of view—often even conflicting views. This is good; it makes people think.

Let us take an example. Suppose the topic is: Teen-Age Youth.

It could be divided as follows:

Speaker 1: The physical growth of adolescents.
Speaker 2: The emotional development of adolescents.
Speaker 3: Social problems of teen-agers.
Speaker 4: Need for vocational guidance.

Questions from the audience can be directed to any of the speakers at the end, when the total subject has been presented. A symposium is more formal than a panel, but less so than a traditional lecture.

A FORUM

As in the days of ancient Rome, a forum is a public assembly where everyone has a chance to voice his views. It often follows a lecture.

Points to remember:

> The leader should always repeat the question to be sure that everyone has heard it.
>
> The leader should interpose brief summaries from time to time to help people keep the thread of the discussion. Lengthy speeches from the floor should be avoided and speakers kept to a few sentences or to one question.

One problem of a forum is that sometimes a few members of the audience dominate. To avoid this, and to give everyone present a chance to have a say, you might try:

"DISCUSSION 66"

By this means, even large audiences, from fifty to two hundred, can be broken into small groups so that everyone can take part.

The chairman asks three persons sitting in one row to turn around and face the three directly behind them. These six choose a chairman whose job it is to see that each person in the six has a chance to speak; they select another of their members as spokesman, to report back later to the full group. This process of breaking into sixes is repeated all over the room.

Broken down in this way, you can get even large groups to think and participate. Perhaps they discuss "What one question would you like to put to the speaker of the evening?"

At the end of six minutes, you will have a series of questions that have been refined by group consideration. Everyone will listen and be more alert to the answers because everyone will have taken part; each spokesman will put the question for his group.

You can adapt and vary Discussion 66 in a broad variety of ways. You might, for example, ask your own members "What one suggestion would you like to make for next year's program?" Or you could put a broad problem before them, such as "How can we best assimilate the new minority group that is moving into town?"

CIRCULAR RESPONSE

If you have to discuss a touchy subject in your Executive Board or Nominating Committee or with any group of about twelve to fifteen (no more than twenty) people, you might try this technique, which is designed to achieve a consensus of opinion without fireworks or hard arguments.

Seat the group in a circle. The chairman or leader proposes the question to be discussed, whereupon the man or woman on his right has the opportunity to express his views. The person next to him follows. *No one may speak again until his turn comes round once more.*

If you are Number 4, you can comment on the ideas of the leader and speakers 1, 2, and 3, but if Number 5 subsequently says something that annoys you, you have to wait to speak until it is your turn again.

Advantages:

The timid person speaks more freely since his natural right to speak is evident.

The monopolizer has no chance to interrupt and "talk people down."

The extremist is modified in his (her) belligerence by the restraint imposed.

People have time to think before speaking.

Young people or newcomers feel themselves on an equal basis with everyone else.

There are other methods for changing pace, other ways to draw out the thinking and creative suggestions of your members. Once you break the set pattern of lectures and venture into new approaches, you will find new methods for yourselves.

How to Interest People in What You Are Doing

WHY BOTHER?

1. So you can attract volunteers.
2. So you can "spark" other people to do similar constructive work needed in the community.
3. So you can raise funds more easily.
4. So your work becomes known to municipal government or others in a position to carry it on and extend it.

You will of course, use different methods depending on your goals.

METHODS

Routine ways in which to keep the community informed of your work on a regular month-by-month basis include:

Newspapers.
Radio.
Speakers at public meetings of other organizations.
Displays and exhibits.
News bulletins; mailings, etc.
Word of mouth (enthusiasm is catching).

You should keep in touch with every group in your community steadily and regularly, not just when you want them for something specific; the more you know of each other's work, the more you can do together.

NEWSPAPER HINTS

Names may "make the news" but avoid personal prestige stories unless the organization's story is also included.

To avoid confusion, one person should be assigned to handle an organization's newspaper and radio contacts. This person should be able to:

Point up the main idea clearly.
Give facts accurately and briefly.
Answer questions of policy and procedure.

When giving out a story, you must:

Type and double-space all copy, using a good ribbon.

Write on one side of the page; keep a carbon of *all* stories.

Know the papers' deadlines; get copy in well in advance.

All copy should include five "W"s in the opening paragraphs:

Who—Who the group is; who presided; who spoke; who made newsworthy proposals.
What—What was the subject of the meeting?
Where—Tell them exactly, using the full address.
When—Exact time and full date.
Why (or How)—What is behind the story? Why did it take place? What is the significance? Why should anyone be interested?

HELPING PHOTOGRAPHERS

Call them up the day before to remind them.

Think up ideas for photos that are a bit out of the ordinary.

Have the key people present and ready (never more than two or three).

Have names and addresses and titles ready to make the caption.

DON'T PLAY FAVORITES

Community papers, language papers, shopping newssheets, etc., reach people too. Don't play only for the big newspapers to get your story across.

PRESS CHAIRMAN

She should know the people with whom she works.

She should call on:

Managing Editor.
City or News Desk Editor.
Woman's Editor.
Radio News Desk.
Radio Women's Commentator.

These personal visits:

Give the new chairman facts she needs such as deadlines, how to route release, policy on photos, etc.
Acquaint her with the people with whom she'll work.
Demonstrate to the editors that she is a responsible person with whom they can work.

TO ACHIEVE COMMUNITY GOODWILL

Be very careful to give credit where credit is due.

Be generous with public thank-you's and appreciation.

Be patient in explaining the work and procedures of your organization.

Be ready to co-operate with other community groups in every possible way. Don't worry lest you lose "position" or "prestige" by this; you will gain, not lose.

RADIO INTERVIEWS

If you are going to be interviewed on radio or TV:

Know what it is you want to get across. You can get across only one or two basic ideas in a brief interview. What do you want these points to be?

Be ready with one (or possibly two) really appropriate stories that illustrate your points in an amusing, relaxed way. You will feel better and you will get your point across better by an anecdote than by a speech.

Know your subject; wait for the questions; don't panic; don't talk too long at any one time. Pretend you are telling just one person what you want to say. Maybe only one is listening anyway! But he or she is important. Persuade that one.

Pitfalls to Avoid

Every organization is confronted with certain problems. Frequently these arise from personality problems. We all know Mrs. Important, Mrs. Sensitive, Mrs. Objector. It takes skillful leadership to keep memberships functioning in a positive direction, avoiding internal conflicts that can undermine over-all objectives.

A group of Korean clubwomen analyzed the main trouble spots in their organizations. This is what they said:[1]

STRUCTURE

One of the most serious defects lies in being top-heavy; everything too often comes from the top, on direction from a few superiors, rather than developing in accordance with the desires of the majority of members. When this happens, groups lack independence, individuality, and their members' support.

Many groups think that a large organization is necessarily better than a small one. Others believe that having a prominent person at the helm guarantees success. They do not ask how great is her dedication, nor that of the members. Sometimes, dazed by important names, they select an outsider as their leader who knows (or cares) nothing of the organization. It would usually be better to elect from their own membership. Nominal leaders seldom find time to study the problems at hand; they are therefore superficial. Because of this, the organization itself becomes a superficial, social affair, rather than a creative, useful body. When leaders think that organizations "belong" to them, and are theirs to dictate, instead of realizing that the groups belong to the members, they remove the value and vitality of the members.

If it is weak, an organization easily dissolves into a body which follows orders blindly from the authorities; bureaucracy prospers. Members gather only to meet and exchange gossip with their friends, rather than to take part in useful work. When members lack original ideas themselves, these can easily be supplied by people with political motives.

LEADERSHIP

If leaders are too stubborn to listen to good advice from their followers, they frequently lose their best members who, though critical, are often able. The figureheads can find no time to study pending problems, therefore their organization becomes meaningless.

In countries where women have long been accustomed to being dependent on patriarchs, they cannot display creative ability when asked to express themselves in discussions. They are prepared only to obey orders from superiors. They need practice.

Women often oppose each other merely for emotional reasons without real differences of opinion. If they oppose, they do not hesitate to leave their associations to form new ones, but since these are created for spite, not more purpose, they are empty.

All these problems arise from leaders thinking the organizations *belong* to them, rather than recognizing that they should be shared with all members. To prosper, an organization must have concrete plans, based on reality and a critical attitude towards their own accomplishments. Otherwise, they attain nothing useful.

WHAT IS NEEDED?

Directors should be trained.

Members should take pride in participating, and not be always silent. Discussions help to produce able leaders.

Opportunities should be made for young women to have room for their own personal tastes and interests, so that the young will join.

Recruiting drives in which members are almost forced to bring in new members should be replaced by efforts to enlist women through interest, desire, and a sense of community spirit.

Measures that are considered good should be put into actual practice, no matter how small they may seem at first.

If people would admire a woman who does a good job, rather than one who holds many empty titles, the pressure of public opinion could make useful changes. Leaders should take one or two substantial posts and fill them sincerely.

How to Make a Budget . . . and Find the Funds

HOW TO MAKE A BUDGET[1]

Before you go out to raise money, a budget must be carefully made. This becomes the goal for your appeal.

A budget must include estimates of:

COST OF OPERATING

Salary for paid secretary or staff (if such exists).
Administration costs:
Rent, light, heat, maintenance.
Telephone and supplies.
Equipment (furniture, typewriters).
Postage.
Insurance and accounting services.

COST OF PROGRAM

This varies, but might include costs of a bulletin, or occasional reports, necessary travel, funds for meetings, etc.

WHERE DO YOU BEGIN?

You can begin with the money you expect as income, and cut your program to fit that.

Or you can study the work that needs doing, your own

group's capacities, and the probable cost of doing what you want to do, then go out to raise enough money to proceed.

Most groups start with their ambitions, then find the funds.

WHO DECIDES?

A special Budget Committee prepares a tentative budget; this is presented to the full Board for discussion and approval; it is then presented to the total membership.

It should show, in three columns:

1. The budget items of the previous year.
2. The actual expenditures under each item.
3. The amounts proposed for the following year, including new items.

Once adopted by the full membership, the budget becomes the basis for the year's expenditures; any changes of major proportions would need to come before the membership again, although bills authorized by the budget need not come up again to the Board.

HOW TO FIND THE FUNDS

There are four major approaches:

1. *Appeals through mass media*: Radio, press, advertising media are constantly being used to create a "climate of opinion," an awareness of needs, and a backdrop against which appeals for community funds can be effective.

   These may be public health drives: polio, blindness, reduction of infant mortality, etc. Or they may be appeals for orphans, widows, or refugees; or hospital campaigns, or book drives for schools.
2. *Individual appeals on a person-to-person basis*: These

may be haphazard, with people standing on the street shaking a can and asking for pennies; or they may be carefully prepared by well-trained, well-informed workers using a previously compiled list of prospects. This is a slow and difficult method, but has been found to be the most effective in helping to enlist the interest and support of an ever-growing number of civic-minded men and women. Once such people become really interested in your undertaking, they generally continue to give thought, energy, and time, as well as money, on a long-term basis.

This type of money-raising can be thought of as a public education campaign, as well as fund-raising.

3. *Fund-raising devices*: Bazaars, benefit performances, and the like may or may not carry with them an effort to educate the donors to the project at hand. It is advisable to use every possible opportunity to develop a sense of community responsibility by helping people to understand your purpose and your goals.
4. *Appeals for large contributions*: Certain types of fund-raising concentrate on major business and industrial concerns, unions, major citizens groups, foundations, and the like. (We are not concerned here with the question of government funds.)

Because most of our readers are working through local and community organizations, we will concentrate on the two areas of:

Individual appeals.
Local fund-raising devices.

INDIVIDUAL APPEALS

The League of Women Voters of the United States has done considerable study of this method, which they use as their basis of support. To them we are indebted for this section. They say that according to their experience, paying personal visits to selected individuals during a short, intensive period is "the best method yet devised" for sound financing of annual budgets. They believe that an organization which is meeting a recognized need in the community and nation, and which presents its needs intelligently and constructively, will find support.

A number of volunteer workers can be trained to work carefully over lists of potential donors, keeping the lists up to date and adding to it. The giving should be spread over a constantly growing number of friends whose good will and encouragement will mean additional support for the work.

The League's experience leads it to say that "personal calls are far more effective than letters; no matter how well written the letters are, the number of prospects who respond to a friendly call is greatly in excess of those who answer by mail."

The collectors should be carefully trained; this is extremely important. Training will bring confidence; it will help volunteers to be convincing and clear; they should know the facts about new plans, the budget, past expenditures, and such details so they can answer well if searching questions are raised.

Their training should give them a sense of pride; they should not feel that they are begging, but rather that they are giving people a chance to support something worthwhile.

Collectors should be chosen on the basis of their ability to make friendly relations with people and to interpret the organization clearly and accurately. Each should have a kit, including specific information and a copy of the budget.

FUND-RAISING DEVICES

Food sales, dances, fashion shows, bazaars, and entertainments are used everywhere in order to raise money. But sometimes these ideas get stale; sometimes a fresh approach is helpful. The following are suggestions gathered from all over the world by the Committee of Correspondence:

SALES

An American girls' college supports a full scholarship by selling boxes of spring flowers to plant early in the season.

A "Swap Sale" can be handled like this: To be admitted you pay a small entrance fee and must also bring an item to exchange. In order to trade, you purchase a "permit" for a tiny sum. The best items change hands many times, bringing in many small coins for the cause; participants often get extremely nice items for mere pennies; everybody has fun.

Balloon Sale. The Swiss wrote that they had great success in selling balloons with a tag attached, giving the address of the purchaser, who let it soar into the air. A substantial prize was offered for the balloon reported from the furthest distance.

Other ideas:

Next-to-New Sale.
Outgrown Exchange (toys, clothes).
Bring-and-Buy Sale (good for cakes).
Book Exchanges.

VARIATIONS ON FASHION SHOWS

Mother-Daughter shows.
Shoe shows.
Modeling coiffures.

AUCTIONS

Refurbished Furniture. An energetic Canadian wanted to raise money for refugee relief. First of all, he persuaded a number of young men with trucks to volunteer a day's work apiece. Then, with the aid of radio and newspapers, he persuaded hundreds of householders to donate a piece of old furniture to be auctioned, assuring them that they would have a percentage of the profit made by its sale. Other volunteers refinished, mended, and painted the furniture; a professional auctioneer offered his services. The auction was such a success that it has become an annual event.

Talent Auction. Not all communities have goods to donate; but all communities have skills to offer. These can be auctioned:

I will read aloud for four hours to someone ill or old.
I will plow three acres.
I will take a child's photo and enlarge it.
I will draw up a will.

Each offer is written on a piece of paper, with the name and address of the donor. The contributions are auctioned; often a tidy sum is raised with no penny of cost involved. Sometimes such an auction serves as a membership drive as well, for people become interested in what you are doing when they work with you.

Giving Up a Meal. "Family Fasting Day" in Austria, "Austerity Day" in England, "Refugee Meal Day" in Canada are all examples of the idea of giving up meals and donating the money saved to a cause. The sponsoring organization usually estimates a given amount for each meal. A less expensive one is served and the difference is contributed.

Fun Can Bring Funds. Norway does it with fishing competitions. Competitors pay a fee to enter; prizes are given both for the largest fish and for the greatest number caught.

In Italy, a ladies club took advantage of the crowded week of the Agricultural Show. They painted targets on the bottom of the fountain pool and gave prizes to those who hit the bull's-eyes with their coins. The game was a great attraction and they raked in many coins.

Another Norwegian idea was to sell postcards all over the country. Each purchaser wrote his name and address and sent the card to the Norwegian Broadcasting Company. Every day a lucky card was drawn, the winner's name was broadcast, and he won a prize. If your cause is nation-wide, and the radio company will work with you, this is an effective device.

Other ideas:

Community sings—competitions, rounds, contests. Sell cakes to the crowd; take up a collection or charge an entrance fee.
Folk dance competitions.
Hay rides.
Athletic matches.

Occasions of fun between groups, or between nearby villages, can create merriment and camaraderie and at the same time raise funds for needed projects.

CHILDREN CAN HELP TOO

If children are to develop a sense of responsibility for others, there must be ways in which they can learn at an early age to take an active part in the life around them. They can often be of substantial help in fund-raising drives for the community, for U.N.I.C.E.F., for refugees, or for other concerns; they can have fun in the process as well.

Odd Jobs: *Guides, Scouts, and Brownies have done this for years throughout the world—weeding gardens, peeling vegetables, cutting grass, etc. Money earned on a certain day, or during a certain week, is donated to the cause. Shoveling snow, washing cars, raking leaves, walking to school and donating the bus fare are other ways in which children frequently contribute.*

Penny Collections: *Every year in Geneva, Switzerland, a group makes a line by putting small coins along the curb of the sidewalk. Attractive posters call attention to the purpose of the collection; the children take turns calling to passers-by: "Please help lengthen the line." Schools sometimes try to get the line all the way around their playground.*

Shop Days: *In a New Zealand school, Shop Day cleaned them out. Each child brought something to sell; nothing over half a crown (about 25 cents) was allowed. Among the things sold were:*

Two pumpkins, price 6d. each.
Half a gallon of lemonade, at 3d. a glass.
Old woolen clothes that had shrunk—ideal for dolls.

Trains: *Nobody really grows up. A toy store loaned a set of electric trains to a group in the United States, who set it up in a railroad station.*

Volunteers took two-hour shifts. For a small fee they would turn on the current for two minutes per customer. The trains flew around the tracks, lights flashing, bells ringing.

Not only children but hurrying adults stopped, fascinated, to watch. They kept contributing coins all day long to keep the trains moving.

Who Is a Leader?

"A LEADER is a person who helps people to get something done —not one who does it herself."

How does a leader get other people to work?

There are six basic ways:

1. Force.
2. Fear.
3. Authority: "I must see that these people produce."
4. Persuasion: "I must get these people to *want* to produce."
5. Rewards.
6. Satisfactions.

There are at least five major desires that impel human beings. These are:

1. Security.
2. Recognition and approval.
3. Influence.
4. Opportunity.
5. Sense of belonging.

Most people want to count for something; they want tomorrow to be better than today; they want to feel a part of something bigger than themselves.

The behavior of a leader has great effect on the spiritual and mental growth of the people around him (or her).

A leader can say autocratically "you are right" or "you are wrong," putting a subordinate in his place with a gesture and leaving no room for comment. Or, in the same situation, he can ask questions, discuss the answers, seek out further opinions. If he uses the latter method, he helps the less-experienced person to develop; he extends his self-respect by giving him room for growth; he implies that his ideas are worth listening to; he helps him to stretch both his horizons and his confidence.

A good leader:

Listens.
Has frequent meetings with his group to develop a united feeling.
Encourages his staff to reach thoughtful conclusions.
Allows discussion and open criticism.
Fosters the fullest participation from everyone, at every level.

A good leader is always conscious of training new leadership among the members; he shares responsibility so that many people within the group have a growing knowledge of all aspects of the work, therefore a growing capacity.

A person has *not* been a really good leader if, within the group, he or she remains the only one capable of holding responsibility. Marks of leadership are:

Willingness to delegate responsibility.

Willingness to step down at the end of an allotted term of office, so as to give new people and new ideas a chance.

Qualities for Good Volunteer Service

By Begum Liaquat Ali Khan, of Pakistan[1]

1. *A genuine love of people*—toleration should spring from compassion, not from indifference; it should be active, not passive.
2. *A mind that is ever open to learning*, even if it does consider itself well-stocked. It is good to remember that what some of us don't know is very profitable to others.
3. *An intense personal faith* in one's work and in the people it concerns. Many people fancy they can convince others without holding any sincere convictions themselves. They simply cannot.
4. *A desire to give and to seek co-operation.* The "lone ranger" attitude makes good movie material but not good social volunteer material. It is better to remember that there are always men and women who can help you, and to give them a chance to do it.
5. *The spirit and courage which can dare to experiment*—by all means look before you leap, but if you are going to leap, don't look too long.
6. *An ability to look and plan ahead, to use initiative in tackling a job*—in other words, don't always wait for

necessity to mother invention; see what you can do about it yourself, and ahead of time.

7. *The ability to infect others with enthusiasm.* It is not enough merely to have conviction and enthusiasm oneself; one must communicate it to others. The world loses much by indifference. It is the job of the social worker to create divine discontent.
8. *A willingness to revise ideas and plans where necessary*—to cut off dead branches and graft on new shoots. We are apt to become so involved, physically and emotionally, in our own ideas and plans and projects, that we forget to be objectively critical of them, or to notice the march of fresh knowledge and ideas. A worker should not be "too busy" to sit back and think sometimes.
9. *The ability to reduce work and situations to simple terms of action, speech, and approach.* This is not as easy as it sounds, but it is the best method for getting results. There are two ways of going about everything. One is complex; the other is simple. Both volunteers and "clients" are frightened off or unnecessarily hampered by words and jargon and schemes which are too technical, complicated, and high-sounding.
10. *Tenacity of purpose*—the reason the bulldog wins is because he "hangs on." That is what a social worker must learn to do too. Hang on, in spite of frustrations and setbacks, and win through.

Proverbs

SOMETIMES when speeches are to be made or lectures prepared, it is helpful to have some neat quotes to help one get ideas across. In the hope that some of the following may be useful, they are included.[1]

PROVERBS

Ashanti, from Ghana

The moon moves slowly, but it crosses the town.
When a man is coming towards you, you need not say "Come Here."
No one tests the depth of a river with both feet.
He who hunts two rats, catches none.

Congo

No matter how full the river, it still wants to grow.
Love is like a baby: it needs to be treated tenderly.
A little subtleness is better than a lot of force.

Ethiopia

Cactus is bitter only to him who tastes of it.
A cat may go to a monastery, but she still remains a cat!
What one hopes for is always better than what one has.

Guinea

Knowledge is like a garden: if it is not cultivated, it cannot be harvested.

Rwanda

If you are building a house and a nail breaks, do you stop building, or do you change the nail?

Senegal

A healthy ear can stand hearing sick words.
The opportunity that God sends does not wake up him who is asleep.

Sierra Leone

To try and to fail is not laziness.
A paddle here, a paddle there–the canoe stays still.

Uganda

A roaring lion kills no game.

Russia

If we knew beforehand where we were going to fall, we could lay down a carpet.
If you don't crack the shell, you can't eat the nut.
Even a blind horse can pull the cart, if he is led.
A spoon of tar will spoil a cask of honey.

❀

Notes

CHAPTER ONE

[1] Dr. Mohei-el-Din Saber, "Obstacles Delaying the Progress of Community Development Programmes in the Arab World," in *Studies in Community Development in the Arab States,* p. 6. Arab States Training Centre for Education for Community Development, Sirs-el-Layyan, U.A.R., 1962.

[2] Letter to Author dated November 11, 1962, from Mrs. Insil Moon of Seoul, Korea.

[3] Pannini Rudaravanija in a speech made before the Asia Society, New York, November 30, 1962.

[4] Malcolm N. Quint, "The Idea of Progress in an Iraqui Village," *Middle East Journal,* Vol. 12, Fall 1958, No. 4, pp. 373–374.

[5] Paraphrase of unpublished notes of group meetings of women in Malaysia, April and May 1963.

CHAPTER TWO

[1] Remarks made at Conference of Women Leaders held at Dacca, East Pakistan, January 1960.

[2] Anonymous Malaysian woman in letter to Author dated April 1962.

[3] 1960 Seminar on Participation of Women in Public Life, Addis Ababa, Ethiopia, December 1960. United Nations, New York, 1961.

[4] Morroe Berger, *The Arab World Today.* Doubleday and Co., Inc., New York, 1962. Copyright © 1962 by Morroe Berger.

[5] *Ibid.,* p. 153.

[6] Melissa Redfield, *Freedom to Discover One's Best and Truest Self.* U.S.I.A. Story no. AH62–81, p. 20. Washington, D.C., November 21, 1962.

[7] Morton M. Hunt, *Her Infinite Variety: The American Woman as Lover, Mate and Rival.* New York, Harper, 1962, p. 91. Copyright © 1962 by Morton M. Hunt.

[8] Letter to Author, Spring 1962, from Zena Kumar, Professor at Delhi University.

[9] *Notes for Women Delegates to the 13th General Assembly* (of the United Nations). Committee of Correspondence, New York, 1958.

[10] Letter to Author from Marjorie Thomson, dated April 7, 1965.

[11] Remarks made at Committee of Correspondence Seminar, April 1960, by Hannah Kassambala of Dar-es-Salaam, Tanganyika.

[12] Speech made by Tani Sisa of Papua at Second South Pacific Conference, Nouméa, 1953, reported in *South Pacific Commission Quarterly Bulletin,* April 1959, p. 24.

[13] *Report of the First Kenya Women's Seminar: The Role of African Women—Past, Present and Future,* Limuru, Kenya, May 1962. Plenary Resolution, p. 17.

CHAPTER THREE

[1] Dr. C. E. Beeby, "Education in Emergent Countries," in *Report of the Annual Meeting of the British Association for the Advancement of Science,* Norwich, England, 1961.

[2] Dr. J. Roby Kidd, "UNESCO at the Crossroads: Continuing Education and the Development Decade." Speech delivered at the N.G.O. Conference on Information about U.N.E.S.C.O., New York, 1961.

[3] George V. Allen, "Education for Progress," Plenary Agenda Item IIIA, World Food Congress, Washington, D.C., June 1963.

[4] *Ibid.*

[5] Dr. Richard Glenn Gettell, "A Plea for the Uncommon Woman," New York *Herald Tribune,* December 22, 1957.

[6] Comments made in seminar discussion, Kampala, Uganda, February 1958.

[7] *Ibid.*

[8] Comments made in seminar discussion, Isfahan, Iran, August 1963.

[9] Letter to Committee of Correspondence from Miss Sylvia Gray, dated June 29, 1959.

[10] Mrs. Chu-Sheng Yeh Cheng, remarks made to Author, March 1963.

[11] Isla Bunbery, *African Women,* Vol. IV, No. 3, December 1961, p. 51.

[12] George V. Allen, *Ibid.*

CHAPTER FOUR

[1] Madame Pandit, of India. From speech before National Council of Women of U.S.A., New York, April 5, 1962.

[2] Patience J. Hamilton, Sierra Leone, Committee of Correspondence Bulletin No. 74, June 1961.

[3] Miss Marion Doro, Ph.D., Ford Foundation grantee for Research on Kenya Legislative Council. Speech "Women Work through Government," given at First Kenya Women's Seminar, May 5–11, 1962, Limuru Conference Center, Kenya.

[4] Committee of Correspondence Bulletin No. 46, September 1957.

[5] Remark made by anonymous West African in conversation with Author.

[6] *Women Are People*, Committee of Correspondence booklet, New York, June 1960, pp. 3–4.

[7] *Ibid.*, p. 4.

[8] Marjorie Tait, *The Education of Women for Citizenship*, U.N.E.S.C.O., Paris, 1954, p. 68.

[9] *Women Are People, Ibid.*, p. 4.

[10] Prime Minister of Iran, comments, August 1956, as quoted in *Women and the Near East* by Ruth Frances Woodsmall. Middle East Institute, Washington, D.C., 1960.

[11] Remarks made to Author by Prime Minister Balewa, Summer 1958.

CHAPTER FIVE

[1] Remarks made by group member at Mothers' Union meeting, Lagos, Nigeria, January 1958.

[2] *Women Are People, Ibid.*, p. 6.

[3] Committee of Correspondence Bulletin No. 56, December 1958, p. 6.

[4] *Latin-American Report*, Vol. V, No. 5, December 1963. International Trade Mart, New Orleans.

[5] *World Health Magazine*, Vol. XV, No. 2, March–April 1962, p. 11. World Health Organization, Geneva, Switzerland.

[6] "Food and People," *U.N.E.S.C.O. Courier*, July–August 1962, No. 7–8, p. 45.

[7] Ritchie Calder, *Common Sense about a Starving World*, Macmillan, New York, 1962, p. 167.

[8] Remarks to Author in private conversation, Summer 1963.

[9] Paraphrase of unpublished notes of group meetings of women in Malaysia, April and May 1963.

[10] Remark to Author by Mrs. Aziza Hussein, Summer 1963. Quoted by permission.

[11] Resolutions, Recommendation and Statements adopted at the General Assembly of the International Council of Women, Washington, D.C., June 1963.

[12] Committee of Correspondence Bulletin No. 38, December 1956.

[13] Remarks made in conversation with Author, July 1961, by Staff of Norwegian Housewives Association.

CHAPTER SIX

[1] Esther Peterson, "American Women at Work," *The American Review,* Vol. II, No. 1, December 1961. (Published quarterly under auspices of the European Center of American Studies of the Johns Hopkins University, Bologna Center, Via Belmeloro 11, Bologna, Italy.)

[2] Dr. Helga Pross, "The Position of Women in a Modern Society," *Journal of Family Welfare,* Vol. VIII, No. 3, March 1962, p. 20. Family Planning Association of India, Bombay.

[3] Dr. Mohei-el-Din Saber, "Obstacles Delaying the Progress of Community Development Programmes in the Arab World," *Ibid.,* p. 30.

[4] Report to the Governments of Ceylon, India, Indonesia, Japan, Pakistan, The Philippines, and Thailand on Conditions of Women's Work in Seven Asian Countries. International Labour Organization, Geneva, Switzerland, 1958.

[5] Paraphrased from letter to Author from Mrs. Zahia Marzouk, Director of Social Welfare, Alexandria, Egypt, dated 31 December 1961. Used with permission.

[6] Mrs. Rita de Bruyn Ouboter, "Women's Employment and Family Life," *Bulletin of International Council of Social Democratic Women,* Vol. XIII, No. 7–8, July–August 1962.

[7] Dr. Helga Pross, *Ibid.,* pp. 24–25.

[8] Mrs. Millicent C. McIntosh, final President's Report at Barnard College, 1962. As quoted in the New York *Times,* November 13, 1962.

[9] Elina Huttunen in conversations at Committee of Correspondence Seminar, New York, April 1960.

[10] Y.W.C.A. Conference at Seoul, Korea, 1960.

CHAPTER SEVEN

[1] John Charles Roche, *Report of the First Kenya Women's Seminar, Ibid.,* p. 31.

[2] *Seminar on the Civic Responsibilities and Increased Participation of Asian Women in Public Life*, Bangkok, August 5–16, 1957. United Nations, New York, 1957.

[3] Ruth Woodsmall, *Women and the New East, Ibid.*, p. 274.

[4] Mrs. Suleiman, Dean of Girls' College, Heliopolis, Cairo, U.A.R., in a conversation with Author, Summer 1963.

[5] Daniel F. McCall, "Korforidua: A West African Town." *Journal of Human Relations,* Vol. VIII, Nos. 3 and 4, Spring and Summer 1960, p. 423. Published at Central State College, Wilberforce, Ohio.

[6] T. S. Tan, "New Trend in Jobs: Preference to Women," *Sunday Times* of Malaya, August 26, 1962.

CHAPTER EIGHT

[1] John W. Gardner, "Can We Count on More Dedicated People?" *Life* magazine, Vol. 48, No. 23, June 13, 1960, p. 100*ff*. Copyright © 1960 by Time Inc. Used with permission.

[2] *Freedom from Hunger Campaign News,* August 1962.

[3] Letter to Author from Mrs. Zahia A. Marzouk, Fall 1962.

[4] Conversation with Author, Summer 1960.

[5] Paraphrase of letter to Author from Miss Lisa Mattson, dated January 1, 1963.

[6] Gift Coupon Program Publication, Project No. 344, Upper Volta. U.N.E.S.C.O., New York.

[7] New Year's Message, December 31, 1953. U.N. Secretariat, SG 1360, Department of Public Information Press Releases, 1953.

[8] John W. Gardner, *Ibid.*, p. 100.

CHAPTER NINE

[1] Dr. Eduard C. Lindeman, "Why They Do It," Speech made at the Session of the Advisory Committee on Citizen Participation on Motivations of Volunteers in Community Service. At National Conference of Social Work, Cleveland, Ohio, June 16, 1949.

[2] Bradford Smith, *Why We Behave Like Americans,* J. B. Lippincott Company, Philadelphia, 1957, p. 104–105. Copyright © 1957 by Bradford Smith.

[3] Dag Hammarskjöld, Address at the University of Lund, Sweden, May 4, 1959, as reported in the New York *Times* Magazine, September 16, 1962.

[4] Dr. Eduard C. Lindeman, "Leadership in Voluntary Enterprise," published for the Council of National Organizations, Oceania Publications, Dobbs Ferry, N.Y., 1948, pp. 76–77.

[5] Alexis de Tocqueville, *Democracy in America*, Henry Reeve text, as revised by Francis Bowen, edited by Phillips Bradley. New York, Alfred A. Knopf, 1960, Vol. I, p. 196. Copyright 1945 by Alfred A. Knopf, Inc.

[6] Adapted from Report on the Role of Specific Ministries and Services in Comprehensive National Community Development Programs, by Glen Leet. New York, Community Development Foundation, June 25, 1962, pp. 45–46.

[7] *Ibid.*, p. 7.

[8] As reported to Author at W.V.S. Headquarters, London, Summer 1962.

[9] Begum Liaquat Ali Khan, Speech before Tenth International Conference of Social Work, Rome, January 1961, as reported in Committee of Correspondence Bulletin No. 73, May 1961, p. 1.

CHAPTER TEN

[1] Paraphrase from essay by Miss Tsugi Shiraishi, Urawa City, Japan, dated 1960, for the Committee of Correspondence, New York.

[2] *Report of the Conference of Women's International Non-Governmental Organizations, March 3–16, 1962*, Committee of Correspondence, New York, 1962.

[3] Marjorie Tait, *The Education of Women for Citizenship*, U.N.E.S.C.O., Paris, 1954, p. 76.

[4] *Ibid.*, p. 77. Italics are the Author's.

[5] Conference, September 1960, of Women Delegates to the Fifteenth General Assembly, United Nations, 1960.

[6] Begum Liaquat Ali Khan in speech before All Pakistan Women's Association, March 3, 1963, Dacca, Pakistan. As reported in *The Morning News*, Dacca, 4 March, 1963.

CHAPTER ELEVEN

[1] "City Students Earn 10 Million in Cooperative School Program," New York *Times*, 24 September, 1963.

[2] Joseph Adejunmobi Adegbite, "Youth Organizations in Africa," in *Journal of Human Relations*, Vol. 8, Nos. 3 and 4, Spring and Summer 1960, p. 721. Central State College, Wilberforce, Ohio.

[3] Committee of Correspondence Bulletin No. 38, December 1956, p. 4.

CHAPTER TWELVE

[1] Dr. Arnold Toynbee, Speech made at Grinnell College, Grinnell, Iowa, February 19, 1963, as quoted in *Christian Science Monitor*, February 20, 1963.

[2] Presidential Address to the Swedish Academy, Stockholm, December 20, 1957, as quoted in the New York *Times*, September 16, 1962.

[3] Paraphrase of letter from Chinese woman of Singapore to Author, 29 August, 1963.

[4] Barbara Ward. Used with permission.

HOW TO GO ABOUT IT: THE ORGANIZATION

[1] *New Hope for Audiences,* Copyright 1954 by National Congress of Parents and Teachers, 700 North Rush Street, Chicago 11, Illinois, is the source for material in this section (pp. 174–179). Used with permission.

PITFALLS TO AVOID

[1] Meeting of Y.W.C.A., Seoul, Korea, February 1960.

HOW TO MAKE A BUDGET

[1] The material in this section (pp. 187–195) has been paraphrased from *How to Find the Funds,* compiled by G. Alison Raymond for the Committee of Correspondence, New York, February 1962.

QUALITIES FOR GOOD VOLUNTEER SERVICE

[1] Quoted from speech made by Begum Liaquat Ali Khan at the Tenth International Conference of Social Work, Rome, January 1961, as reported in Committee of Correspondence Bulletin No. 73, May 1961, p. 4.

PROVERBS

[1] In this section the African proverbs come from *African Proverbs,* compiled by Charlotte and Wolf Leslau, Copyright © 1962 by the Peter Pauper Press, Mount Vernon, New York, and the Russian proverbs from *Russian Proverbs,* Copyright © 1960 by the Peter Pauper Press. Used with permission.